Games as Texts

Games as Texts

A Practical Application of Textual Analysis to Games

Alayna Cole
Dakoda Barker

CRC Press
Taylor & Francis Group
Boca Raton London New York

CRC Press is an imprint of the
Taylor & Francis Group, an **informa** business

First Edition published 2021
by CRC Press
6000 Broken Sound Parkway NW, Suite 300, Boca Raton, FL 33487-2742

and by CRC Press
2 Park Square, Milton Park, Abingdon, Oxon, OX14 4RN

© 2021 Taylor & Francis Group, LLC

CRC Press is an imprint of Taylor & Francis Group, LLC

ISBN: 978-0-367-34802-1 (hbk)
ISBN: 978-0-367-35428-2 (pbk)
ISBN: 978-0-429-33132-9 (ebk)

Typeset in Minion
by Deanta Global Publishing Services, Chennai, India

Contents

Acknowledgements

Games as Texts was influenced by a university course originally written and developed by Ginna Brock. All information and ideas are used with permission.

Introduction

WHEN WE WERE TEACHING game design to undergraduate students, we had the pleasure of lecturing in a course dedicated to game analysis. Most students walked into the classroom in the second half of their second year, exactly halfway through their degrees. These were students who were passionate about games, had a basic understanding of design principles and programming, and were ready to explore games through in-depth discussions and long-form writing. (Okay, maybe they weren't looking forward to the writing; they were undergraduate students, so that's to be expected.)

When we started having conversations and reading assignments, we realised that teaching students how to analyse games has to involve more than just teaching them the difference between structuralism and post-structuralism. Although our students were passionate about games, in many cases they lacked faith that games were worth talking about beyond calling them 'good' or 'bad' and giving them scores. We had to teach them that games are cultural artefacts worthy of the same attention as novels, poems, theatre, film, paintings, and other texts.

But what do we mean by 'texts'? Although textual analysis is often associated with literal *text*—like novels or poems—Barthes (1957) describes 'texts' as all artefacts and activities of human expression. This can, for example, include the written and performative aspects of a play (Fernández-Vara 2014: 5–6) or the entirely non-written, non-verbal expression of a painting (Belsey 2013). It can also include the interactive experience of a game—be that boardgame, tabletop game, videogame, or another hybrid interactive experience.

By referring to games as 'texts', we are allowing ourselves to engage with them through textual analysis. We are able to use the tools provided to us by other fields who engage with textual analysis and apply them to the games we are playing and creating. In doing so, we can expand our vocabulary for examining games and their social impacts.

Our students knew how to have conversations about the media they engaged with. They had strong opinions about whether or not they liked different games and could articulate why. But the language they were using was the language of game reviews—which is the most common writing that game audiences consume alongside the games they play. Fernández-Vara (2014) suggests that borrowing terms from game reviews means also borrowing terms from marketing materials, which reviews often draw from. Depending on the outlet, games journalism and games public relations can be difficult to differentiate; journalists receive in-depth emails describing the impressive features of games, and we know from our own experience as reviewers that it can be hard to avoid using this language in the reviews we publish.

Game creators and audiences—and the journalists writing these reviews—need more accessible tools and vocabulary (Fernández-Vara 2014: 2) so they can talk about games in a way that better acknowledges their cultural significance beyond their 'impressive graphics' or 'fun systems'. Diverse approaches to game analysis exist, but they are often buried in dense academic papers or are still waiting to be explicitly borrowed from parallel disciplines. The approach we taught in our game analysis class was derived from one such parallel discipline of study: English literature.

The structure of our course originally mirrored the structure of a similar literary studies course at the same university, which uses the analytical lenses in Barry's *Beginning Theory* (2009) as a scaffold. Our book expands on and deviates from the structure of the course from when it was first taught, but its essence is still based on literary theories. These theories are referred to as 'lenses' because they are a screen through which we can observe texts—and the wider world. The idea is that every text can be observed in different ways, each revealing additional depth and impact. By applying literary lenses to games—including the non-exhaustive selection present within this text—we can examine these texts from different angles and within different historical and social contexts.

Descriptions of these lenses can be dense, and it's difficult to encourage a game audience to put aside game reviews and instead engage with games criticism. Although game studies has been around for a surprisingly long time—with John Huizinga's foundational book *Homo Ludens* published as far back as 1938 and the study of ludology starting to be popularised by Gonzalo Frasca in 1999—even undergraduate students are more likely to read a review than a paper presented at the Digital Games Research Association (DiGRA) conference. Varied approaches to game analysis—like the ones presented in this book—need to be made more accessible if we are going to help players and creators alike see games in more nuanced ways.

This is particularly important for theoretical lenses that are focused on the perspectives of social groups and identities. Games have a fraught history with diversity, but diversity is not a new concept, and examining cultural artefacts from identity-based perspectives has been practiced for centuries (Barry 2009: 116). It is impossible for humans to separate themselves from the texts they engage with and if we create more accessible ways to talk about these feelings and perspectives, we may be able to unpack the ongoing arguments that have been happening in the games industry about race, gender, class, disability, mental health, and sexuality.

APPROACH

Each chapter of this book is dedicated to a different lens and the unique perspective it offers for analysing games. However, despite looking at these theories as discrete lenses, we are mindful of the way that each theory has developed in response to the approaches that came before it (Barry 2009: 2). This means each perspective—and the identities that those perspectives reflect—must be considered intersectionally. Intersectionality describes the interconnected nature of social groups and communicates the inherent fallacy of discussing one facet of identity without exploring all facets (Shaw 2015: 7, 239). For example, although a feminist lens allows for interesting gender-based analysis of a text, an analysis is flawed if it considers the experiences of women without also exploring other genders using queer theory, the race of those characters using postcolonialism and race studies, and so on.

Game studies should be inherently good at intersectional approaches because we're used to examining the intersections between ideas. Both the creation and analysis of games have been established by exploring the connections between games and other disciplines. However, the value that each discipline brings to game studies has been an ongoing source of debate between scholars. Most game studies scholars are aware of—and tired of—the 'so-called ludology/narratology debate' (Pearce 2005), which began in the early 2000s. Despite scholars like Frasca (2003) insisting that the debate 'never took place', there is a lack of consensus regarding the degree to which game studies should be influenced by narrative and narratology (Aarseth 2001), and these discussions are ongoing.

Despite the position of some ludologists that narrative should not be considered in game studies—or perhaps that games cannot tell stories at all (Juul 1999)—the theories from which our research methods arise are fundamentally interested in the narrative of games, and we posit that these narratives are worthy of exploration. However, this does not mean that we are positioning ourselves as narratologists in this ongoing debate. Rather, we believe that narratology and ludology cannot truly be separated in games, as the mechanical, dynamic, and aesthetic elements of games (Hunicke, LeBlanc, & Zubek 2004) are inherently linked.

Just as we must understand and position ourselves in relation to debates within game studies, we must also consider our relationship to areas of contention within the field of literary studies. One of these debates examines the place of the author in relation to the work being analysed; the idea that the author can be disconnected from their work is referred to as 'the death of the author' based on Barthes' (1977) book of the same title. Barthes (1977) suggests that disconnecting the author from the text allows the analyst to avoid trying to 'decipher' the text in terms of the context in which it was written and the intentions of the author. While some analysts agree with this approach, others consider intent and the author's historical context integral to the analysis process.

Literary studies has engaged in similar debates about whether the interpretation of the audience should be considered when analysing a text. 'Reader response theory' maintains that meaning is not located in the text but is created through the reader's engagement with it. Stanley Fish suggests that 'the form of the reader's experience, formal units, and the structure of intention are one, that they come into view simultaneously' (in Tompkins 1980: 177), meaning that a text cannot be considered as a 'complete' object if the analyst disregards the audience's experience or the author's intentions.

Debates about the relationship between a text and its creator or its audience are equally valuable—if not more so—when examining game objects. Games are altered more by the impact of the audience than other cultural artefacts—like books and films. This is because games are (typically) static objects unless an audience is interacting with them. Although *Games as Texts* does not put player experience—or related concepts like embodied play (Keogh 2018) and player agency (Cole 2018a)—at the forefront of our analysis, we acknowledge that the player cannot be separated from the game object because its systems cannot be put into motion without an audience.

Analysing a game requires the researcher to look at the game as a system (Fullerton 2004), but also to examine elements of the game as individual components. Analysing games is complex and informative, and, by approaching games as texts through the lenses of literary theories, we intend to elevate games as an artistic craft that produces cultural artefacts rather than simply consumer products. In this way, textual analysis of games fundamentally differs from the value judgements of journalistic game writing that typically intends to review a product rather than engaging with a text for its content and cultural significance.

When players view themselves solely as consumers rather than as individuals appreciating an artistic craft, they form expectations and feel entitled to a product which minimises their understanding of a text's artistic and critical significance. *Games as Texts* seeks to model the application of literary theories to games to make textual analysis more accessible, giving individuals some of the tools and vocabulary they can use to articulate a critical understanding of games.

Games as Texts is primarily designed to aid individuals who are analysing games for research, whether that be for academic publication, tertiary classes, long-form press, or personal enjoyment. We aim to provide historical context around literary theories, as well as definitional information and practical examples that will allow you to apply these theories in your own work. Additionally, *Games as Texts* hopes to demonstrate the role of games as cultural artefacts—either actively or passively—to the academy by showing how games are socially significant and can be analysed as such. Our book also aims to assist players in recognising the potential of games and to assist developers in considering the values that their work conveys (Fullerton 2004).

With our approach established, let's commence our journey into literary theories and textual analysis.

WHEN ANALYSING A GAME USING THESE LENSES, ASK YOURSELF...

At the end of each chapter, we will provide you with some questions that you can use to begin thinking critically about games from the perspective we have been exploring. But it's important to remember that observing representations and ideas within a text is only the first step! Here are some questions that will help you take your observations and turn them into critical analyses.

1. What can you observe and what is it trying to achieve?
2. What techniques are being used in this game and to what end?
3. What do my observations reveal about society?
4. Is this a deliberate commentary or does it reveal subconscious values?
5. What does this* mean?

* In this question, 'this' refers to the observation or argument that you have just made. You can continue asking 'what does this mean?' until you find values and meanings in a text.

CHAPTER 1

Games and Universal Truths

LIBERAL HUMANISM IS INTERESTED in the foundations of a medium, and the foundations of the human story. This theory—or meta-theory—is the basis for all critical analysis of texts. It encourages us to see how all texts have the power to reveal universal human truths (Barry 2009: 17–18). By examining modern texts through this lens, their content can be distilled to reveal the similar themes of the human condition that have always influenced our stories.

Studies suggest that, despite being dressed up in different ways, there are only a small number of plots that are repeated over and over across different mediums of storytelling. There have been many hand-coded and—more recently—computer-coded attempts to trace the similarities between the 'shapes' of plots. Hand-coded attempts have found three (Foster-Harris 1959), seven (Booker 2004), twenty (Tobias 1993), or thirty-six (Polti 1895) common plots. Reagan et al. (2016) completed a thorough computer analysis and found six main emotional arcs and connected these back to oral histories and early folk stories.

No matter the number of similar plots, the important point is that commonalities exist between the stories we tell now and have told throughout history. Although games differ from traditional linear narratives in many ways, liberal humanism suggests that humans have prioritised the same essential ideas throughout history and that these commonalities are more important than the innovations of a medium or of a particular text within that medium (Barry 2009: 17–18).

Liberal humanism invites us to look at commonalities between texts and between people. In doing so, this allows us to remember that we are all human and, despite variations in the specifics of our experiences, we all have the capacity to feel empathy for the fundamental truths underpinning the lives of others. Many of the literary theories we are exploring in this book focus on the differences between social groups and the way that the representations of those identities within texts can reflect reality; these theories are a rebellion against the liberal humanist idea that everybody experiences the world in the same way.

However, in our approach to liberal humanism, we suggest that this theory is not claiming that human beings and their experiences are homogenous but, instead, that focusing on similarities is more important than focusing on differences. This includes the similarities between texts and the ways that they elicit emotion from an audience. For literature, this typically refers to poetic devices. Poetic devices are simply the techniques used by an author to create meaning; you have probably heard of some more common poetic devices like metaphors, similes, personification, alliteration, and so on.

Language can be used to 'enact' what it depicts by taking advantage of the connection between form and meaning (Barry 2009: 19). In literature, this refers to the way that the poetic devices within a text can help to create the meaning of that text. This approach to textual analysis sits parallel to the concept of 'ludonarrative harmony' in game studies, whereby designers try to develop a strong connection between the narrative (meaning) of a game and the mechanics (form) through which that narrative is told (Pynenberg 2012).

Liberal humanism is interested in the ways that language (and mechanics) can enact meaning. As a result, this theoretical approach values the way that a text is 'showing and demonstrating' ideas rather than 'explaining or saying' them (Barry 2017: 19). Many writers have heard this put more simply: 'show, don't tell'. In game design, this idiom is taken one step further and designers are told, 'do, don't show'. This approach to design suggests that, where possible, players should be able to interact with a text—or 'do'—rather than be shown content by the designer in the form of cutscenes, dialogue sequences, and so on. Player agency—or the ability for a player to 'do'—is valued by many developers, and this agency allows players to be the cause within 'the cause-and-effect process that drives a narrative arc' (Cole 2018a).

Viewing game systems through the lens of liberal humanism encourages us to see how the player's actions and interactions are inextricably linked to the messages that a game conveys, in the same way that poetic devices and content are connected in traditional linear narratives. Liberal humanism asks us to look at games through the eyes of the individual interacting with them and, more than that, through the greater human experience and the 'universal truths' presented by them (Barry 2009: 17–18).

ARCHETYPES AND THE MONOMYTH

Archetypes in literature are recurring symbols, characters, and ideas that occur throughout the history of human storytelling. Liberal humanism focuses on connecting modern texts to the archetypes established in foundational stories, thereby situating all texts within the same continuum of storytelling. Thus, having an understanding of different archetypes and being able to identify them in modern texts is an integral aspect of liberal humanist analysis—and remains an important tool when performing all forms of textual analysis.

One of the most well-known archetypal plot structures is the 'monomyth' or 'hero's journey'. In his 1949 book *The Hero with a Thousand Faces*, Joseph Campbell defines the monomyth as a seventeen-stage journey. In short, the monomyth describes a hero's call to adventure, the trials they face on their journey, and their return to their normal life as a changed person. Campbell codified this ur-narrative structure after tracing similarities across mythological stories from around the world. Although the monomyth concerns itself only with early foundational narratives, the structure continues to influence or materialise in modern stories—intentionally and otherwise.

The monomyth is not the only structure by which we can design a game narrative, but those who recommend this story arc praise its 'simplicity' (Dunniway 2000). By scaffolding a game using a narrative structure that everybody is familiar with—either explicitly or implicitly—games can spend 'less time explaining' and move into action quicker (Dunniway 2000). The aptly named *Journey* (Thatgamecompany 2020) was explicitly designed with this in mind (Chen, in Ohannessian 2012). The game relies on the monomyth to guide the player, giving them no explicit instructions about their purpose for traversing the landscape. The landscape itself—more specifically, its topography—mirrors the rise and fall of the hero's

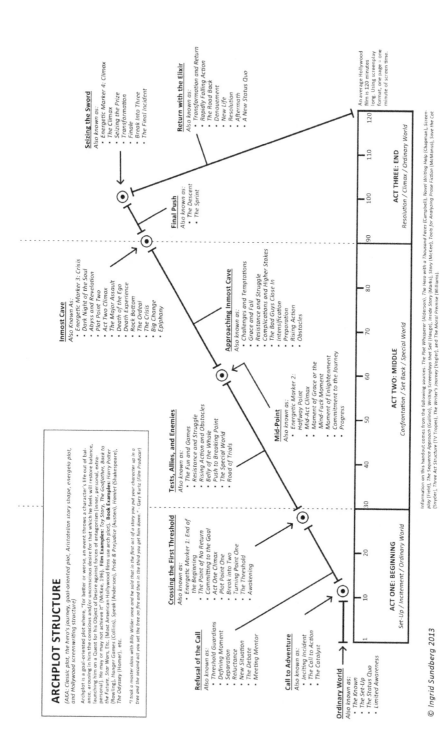

FIGURE 1.1 A visual depiction of the different stages in the hero's journey (Sundberg 2013).

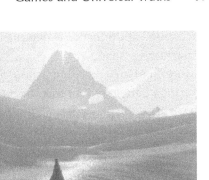

FIGURE 1.2 The player reaches the climax of *Journey* after climbing both a literal and metaphorical mountain (Edwards 2013).

journey as it appears when it is drawn as a diagram of rising and falling tension (Figures 1.1 and 1.2).

One of the reasons *Journey* is so effective is that the player-character receives guidance from an ally. This ally comes in the form of another player who can only communicate with you using body language and short musical sounds. They can choose to guide you through your adventure, showing you the path and extra secrets along the way. An 'ally' is one of several recurring characters within the monomyth narrative structure. Vogler (1998) interpreted the monomyth to define eight character archetypes: hero, mentor, threshold guardian, herald, shapeshifter, shadow, ally, and trickster. Each of these can be found in games, and can be used to guide an analysis through a liberal humanist lens.

For example, early games in the *Pokémon* series (Game Freak 2019) follow this archetypal model closely. In *Red* and *Blue* (1998), the player-character is the 'hero', and they are given the task of adventuring through Kanto to collect Pokémon and eventually defeat the Champion. The task is given by Professor Oak, the 'herald', who also acts as an ongoing 'mentor' for the adventure. Oak's grandson is the player-character's rival and appears intermittently throughout the game, first as an 'ally', but also as a 'shapeshifter' as he reveals himself to be the Champion that the player ultimately has to defeat to win the game. Along the journey, the player-character must gain gym badges from gym leaders—the 'threshold guardians'—and must also defeat members of Team Rocket, who act as the narrative's 'shadow'.

More than a decade later, the *Pokémon* series is still releasing games featuring characters that map to many of the same archetypes, but that also surprise the player by subverting the established archetypes in unexpected ways. In *Sword* and *Shield* (2019), the game still features a professor, but her granddaughter better maps to the 'mentor' archetype throughout the story and becomes a professor at the end of her story arc. This game still has a 'team' of apparent antagonists (this time it's Team Yell), but it turns out they aren't trying to steal Pokémon; their goal is to enthusiastically cheer for one of the other gym challengers and prevent you from stealing her spotlight. Chairman Rose seems like an 'ally' for most of the story, but he is actually a 'shapeshifter' who turns out to be the villain, and his minions are the real 'shadow' of the story.

Pokémon demonstrates a way that many modern stories are inspired by narrative structures and archetypal characters but don't necessarily use every single archetype from a particular model. The series also shows how archetypes can be deliberately subverted, combined, or otherwise modified. By using techniques such as conflating archetypes (so that one character plays multiple roles) or switching archetypes (so that a character you expect to be one archetype turns out to be another), the *Pokémon* series is able to follow a familiar and comfortable formula, while making each story fresh and interesting to a return player.

FAMILIAR FACES IN UNFAMILIAR PLACES

Analysing *Mass Effect* through a Liberal Humanist Lens

Mass Effect (BioWare 2007) uses familiar archetypal characters to allow the player to better connect with a narrative set in unfamiliar galaxies. This analysis will identify the 'hero', 'mentor', 'shadow', and 'threshold guardian' in the story—based on the model developed by Vogler (1998)—as well as explore the purpose of these archetypes within the text.

The hero of *Mass Effect* is Shepard, the player-character and protagonist. Shepard is the first human 'Spectre', who are agents given power to maintain stability throughout the galaxy however they deem necessary. By being the first of their species to be granted this power, Shepard becomes a type of 'Chosen One', as is typical of a character adhering to the hero archetype.

Shepard can have a range of backgrounds based on player choice; however, many of these allow Shepard to adhere to the stereotypical heroic trajectory regardless of the customisation option that the player selects.

Shepard may have been the sole survivor of an attack, an orphan raised on the streets, a brave war hero, or a refugee from a destroyed colony; regardless of the origin story that the player chooses, Shepard is established as a character who has faced adversity and risen above it.

As the hero, the archetypes of other characters are defined through their relationships with Shepard. Captain David Anderson plays the role of 'mentor' to Shepard, and originally was supposed to play the role of Chosen One—the first human Spectre—before being sabotaged and is instead preparing Shepard for the job. Anderson acts as an unwavering supporter of Shepard throughout the game, risking both his career and his life to assist Shepard in their heroic quest. The relationship between Shepard and Anderson is deliberately unambiguous to contrast with the unfamiliar aspects of the setting and institutions—including the Spectres—that the audience needs to understand. This allows the audience to learn about the universe in which *Mass Effect* is set without also immediately being challenged by complicated relationships between characters.

Although supporting Shepard in all aspects of their role as a Spectre, Anderson particularly puts himself at risk to assist them in their pursuit of the narrative's 'shadow'. The 'shadow' role is occupied by two characters—Saren, who is considered a villain from the beginning of the game, and Sovereign, who the player discovers has been influencing Saren to assist with their own mission to eradicate all life in the galaxy.

Both Saren and Sovereign can be considered a 'shadow' to Shepard; however, each serve a different purpose for the audience. Saren is a tangible individual—a straightforward face of the narrative's antagonist that Shepard (and therefore the player) can pursue. Saren is responsible for the betrayal that sabotaged Anderson's attempt to become the first human Spectre, and so the player can easily and unquestioningly be positioned in opposition to Saren from the beginning of the game. He is also established as a foil to Shepard, as the two of them are the only individuals known to have interacted with an ancient and advanced piece of technology called the 'Prothean Beacon' without being killed or losing their sanity.

The tangibility of Saren as an enemy is important because Sovereign—the greater and more dangerous villain in the narrative—is a less tangible force. Initially, Sovereign appears to be a Reaper starship that Saren was somehow able to reactivate; however, as the narrative progresses, it is discovered that Sovereign is actually a fully sentient Reaper who is leading a mission to 'harvest' sentient life and grow their race. It is further revealed that Sovereign uses Saren as a pawn throughout the narrative to aid in this mission using a process referred to as 'indoctrination', complicating their relationship. Saren did not take over a Reaper ship as originally suspected; rather, the ship took over Saren.

Even as this is revealed, Sovereign still takes the appearance of a large starship and so Saren acts as the more straightforward individual enemy while Sovereign is representative of the overarching threat. When Sovereign's influence over Saren dissipates towards the conclusion of the narrative, Saren expresses regret for his actions; however, even despite this remorse he is still depicted as somebody who was a villain made *more* villainous rather than an innocent victim, ensuring his status as 'shadow' remains.

The primary resistance Shepard experiences in their pursuit of both Saren and Sovereign is the Citadel Council. This institution is the narrative's 'threshold guardian'; in addition to being arbiters of who can and cannot be a Spectre, the Council acts as a gatekeeper to Shepard by allowing or disallowing them to pursue both individual and institutional threats. In this way, the Council does not only guard the initial threshold to Shepard's quest but several subsequent thresholds throughout their journey.

Although the Council is an unfamiliar organisation to the player, using archetypes allows the player to draw parallels between the Council's role in *Mass Effect* and the role of 'threshold guardian' characters and groups in other narratives—as well as in their own reality. By adhering to archetypes when establishing the narrative's 'hero' and 'shadow', *Mass Effect* clearly positions the player so that they become frustrated by the Council and the obstacles that they put between Shepard and Saren/Sovereign. *Mass Effect* uses well-established archetypes when introducing its audience to an unfamiliar setting to ensure the player understands who is their ally and who is their adversary while trying to decipher the intricacies of the galaxy they are exploring. This allows the series to build a foundation that can then be subverted in subsequent games set in the same, now-familiar location.

In addition to plots and characters, symbols are a common archetypal element of texts. Symbols are any items or objects that are representative of a larger idea (Barry 2009). They can typically be traced across narratives and connect to the larger sociocultural context in which a text was created. Common symbols are recurring colours (red as love), animals (dove as peace), or settings (garden as paradise).

Colours are an interesting symbol to examine in games because they are able to communicate not only an emotional purpose but a mechanical one—whether it be to denote allies and enemies, symbolise icons in a puzzle, or differentiate levels and spaces. In the *Assassin's Creed* (Ubisoft 2018) series, 'Eagle Vision' can be used to overlay colours onto the world, allowing the protagonist (and player) to distinguish between allies, enemies, and targets based on colour symbolism. Allies are depicted in blue, which is a colour associated with 'good' due to its connection to the sky and heavenly beings; enemies are instead coloured red, which is associated with concepts like war, blood, and anger. *Assassin's Creed* relies on a similar good/bad dichotomy with the white hooded robes of the Assassins and the black outfits of significant Templars (along with their red crosses); white is, again, typically associated with goodness and purity while black is associated with evil and death.

After early *Assassin's Creed* games established the concept that blue/white is good and red/black is evil, the series began to play with these assumptions to create more complex heroes. Later protagonists are more likely to make morally questionable decisions or break the rules of their order, and often do so while wearing darker versions of the Assassin's garb that players of the series have become accustomed to. By using colour to establish stereotypes and obvious binaries and then manipulating colour to demonstrate moral shades of grey, *Assassin's Creed* encourages players to interrogate their assumptions and examine the complexity of reality in a similar way.

EMOTIONS ARE UNIVERSAL

Analysing texts at a macro level to identify the archetypes they use is one way to engage with universal human truths, but it is also valuable to look at the individual experiences of characters and the way they reflect common human concerns. These concerns are often described as the 'themes' of the work; although texts can explore any theme, there are recurring central concepts across texts that express 'ideas that have meaning to many individuals regardless of the time or place' like love, loss, nostalgia, sacrifice, and conflict (Kirszner & Mandell 1993: 3–4).

The narrative of *Bastion* (Supergiant Games 2011) features many of these themes and, in doing so, explores the universal human truths that liberal humanism is used to identify. *Bastion* is set in Caelondia, a city that has been fractured by an event known as the Calamity. A narrator tells the story of the Kid—the player-character and protagonist—who does not speak. The story follows the Kid's loss of innocence, his grief over his home, his uncertainty as he tries to determine which path to follow, and the community he forms with the few other survivors.

The narrative of *Bastion* culminates in a scene underpinned by betrayal and sacrifice: does the Kid save Zulf, who betrayed Caelondia after wrestling with his own loss and uncertainty, or does the Kid choose to protect himself? The individual circumstances of this narrative are fantastical but reflect real-life narratives. The loss of Caelondia reflects the loss of real communities during wars or natural disasters, and the exploration of how we cope with loss and grief can apply to not only these major events that affect large groups but also to events that happen in an individual's life. Narratives about these universal human themes allow us to safely explore our emotions and apply the lessons we learn to our own lives.

Texts allow us to not only explore human emotions in unconventional or fantastical settings but also to explore how universal truths might apply to non-human characters. By asking the audience to imagine how human emotions might be applied to personified animals, fictional species, or sentient artificial intelligence, we are encouraged to step back and look at universal truths from a more objective position. This is achieved in *Nier: Automata* (PlatinumGames 2017), which explores the relationship between humans and machines as a way to ask questions about the universal 'human' experience (Kirszner & Mandell 1993).

Although humans are long extinct in *Nier: Automata*, grand notions about the greatness of humanity remain, defended and preserved by androids that humans created in their image. These androids—whose rallying cry is 'glory to mankind'—wage an endless war against the 'machines'. The machines are considered lesser beings, incapable of profoundly 'human' traits like emotion, self-awareness, or speech. However, the machines are repeatedly shown to be more than simple tools of war: many machines demonstrate advanced speech and thought capabilities, with some choosing to forgo their programmed violent behaviours entirely. For example, Pascal and his village of machines create a peaceful society—forming families, establishing diplomatic relations with other groups, and taking an interest in philosophy. The machines, it turns out, are capable of growth and advancement: they can learn, think, and feel.

Before they became extinct, the humans treated the androids as 'tools' that were useful and incapable of the traits that they considered to be uniquely human. These lessons were internalised by the autonomous androids, who chastise each other for displays of emotion because these feelings are 'prohibited'. In the world of *Nier: Automata*, humans failed to recognise that the universality of emotions extended beyond themselves to other creatures—including those that they created—and inadvertently taught the androids this same lesson. In the game, the androids repeat these mistakes with the machines.

At their essence, the androids and machines are extremely similar. Both were created by a now-extinct species, are artificial intelligences, and are capable of independent thought, emotion, and speech. The fundamental difference between them is that the androids were made in the image of humans while the machines were built by an alien species. If the androids were built to reflect the humans that created them, what does their overall dismissal of the machines as 'lesser' say about humanity?

You can apply a liberal humanist lens to a text by looking for the 'themes' that are considered fundamentally human like love, loss, nostalgia, sacrifice, and conflict (Kirszner & Mandell 1993: 3–4) as well as emotions like joy, grief, rage, and sadness. Who the text allows to express these universal truths, how they are expressed, and the tensions this can cause can be examined to reveal humanity's similarities, idiosyncrasies, or hubris.

WHEN ANALYSING A GAME THROUGH A LIBERAL HUMANIST LENS, ASK YOURSELF...

1. What universal experiences are depicted?
2. Does the text allude to myths, folklore, or religious stories? For what purpose?
3. Does the text try to explain the unexplainable? This might include origin stories, purpose, destiny, the afterlife, etc.
4. How does the text reflect universal hopes, fears, and expectations?
5. How does the narrative follow archetypal structures?
6. How do the characters fit within archetypes?
7. What symbols are in the text? What are they communicating?
8. What are the key themes of the texts, and how do they relate to universal human experiences?
9. What common human situations and feelings are revealed in the text?

CHAPTER 2

Games and Structure

WHEN APPLIED AS A literary theory, structuralism is concerned with the 'structures' of a particular medium and how texts do—or do not—adhere to them. Structuralism as a movement began in the 1950s (Barry 2009: 38) and is concerned with how a text relates to other texts. When performing a structuralist analysis, we are looking for patterns and dualities, as well as the ways that a text connects to genres and other canonical structures that exist outside the text. Structuralism suggests that meaning is always found by examining a text's place within its external context rather than within the text itself (Barry 2009: 38). This theory, at its core, is about the way people construct the world and the 'recognizable and repeated forms' that we design in doing so (Hawkes 1977: 14–15).

Structuralists believe that, through language, people construct themselves and the world they live in. As Hawkes (1977: 14–15) says, 'man constructs the myths, the social institutions, virtually the whole world as he perceives it, and in doing so he constructs himself'. But the gendered language of this quote reveals an issue with structuralism—we cannot state that people construct the structures of society when many groups of people are unwelcome in the process of that construction. The structures that are referred to by structuralists are institutions built by white, able-bodied, cis men. These are the types of contradictions that *post-structuralists* are looking for within texts as they deconstruct them.

Where structuralists seek parallels and reflections in their analysis, post-structuralists look for contradictions, paradoxes, conflicts, and omissions (Barry 2009: 70). Contradictions are inherent in the structures surrounding videogames as a medium. For example, although videogames have existing institutions, like genres, the lines between them are blurry and difficult to define. This chapter will examine how to apply both a structuralist and post-structural lens to games and what each approach is able to reveal.

GENRE

As Lucy Morris stated in her 2019 GCAP talk on genre, 'Genre is such a fluid concept—not any one person can decide what they mean!' For example, the 'first-person shooter' has a range of conventions that are used to define it as a genre—such as weapon-based combat and first-person perspective—but the games that share these traits are so incredibly different that classifying them as part of a single category is not useful. Both *Doom* (id Software 1993) and *Portal* (Valve 2007) are first-person perspective games involving gun-based interactions, but *Portal* doesn't have varied weapons or ammunition. *Superhot* (Superhot Team 2016) is also a first-person perspective game about weapon combat but, mechanically, doesn't function in real time.

Matters are complicated further when 'third-person shooters' are introduced, many of which have identical conventions to some of their 'first-person shooter' cousins and only differ in any significant way through their camera perspective. In fact, 'third-person shooters' can be closer to some 'first-person shooters' than some 'first-person shooters' are to each other. Structural analysis of videogames that attempts to examine genres can quickly become post-structuralist because of the difficulty in meaningfully separating genre categories and examining them as institutions.

Game genres are defined in varied ways. For example, 'first-person shooters' are defined based on their mechanics, but 'horror' games are similar to one another because of their theme and the emotional response they create in a player. It is possible for a game to belong to multiple genres if it includes mechanics and themes that adhere to the conventions of these different categorisations. Other genres, like 'roguelikes', are based on a 'prolific game' (Morris 2019) that they share similarities with. 'Roguelike' literally means 'like *Rogue*' (A.I. Design 1980); although this game was not the first game that used the conventions of the genre, it is exemplary in terms of its procedurally generated dungeon levels, turn-based gameplay, and permanent player-character death. In 2008, the International Roguelike Development Conference sought to codify what a 'roguelike' must have in order to 'properly' conform to the genre conventions; however, this 'official' decision has not stopped the genre being applied to a wide variety of disparate games—or from spawning a related genre, the 'rogue-lite'.

A structural analysis can be applied to determine how a game fits within the conventions of its genre, but also how the structures of that genre create meaning. Viewing roguelikes through a structuralist lens reveals that, although these games are composed of computer-generated levels and random systems, the player experience is created in the ways these systems interact (Ward 2015). In roguelikes like *NetHack* (NetHack DevTeam 1987) and *Caves of Qud* (Freehold Games 2015), symbols are used to create the physical structure of each level and these adhere to conventions that allow the player to make educated guesses about the nature of new symbols they encounter; if roguelikes were completely random, players would not be able to learn the structures that 'persist between playthroughs' (Ward 2015), which reduces the potential for meaning making.

Another genre characterised by a combination of persistent systems and randomised levels is the 'battle royale' genre. This emergent genre became a phenomenon after the launch of *PlayerUnknown's Battlegrounds* (PUBG Corporation 2017), despite several games—and even more game modes and mods—having already established the foundations of the genre before *PUBG*'s launch. The genre at its core is defined by interactions between individuals or squads where each is trying desperately to survive, until somebody is the 'last one standing' and wins the game. With the release of several varied approaches to battle royale games, the other conventions of the genre have become clearer; common conventions include large map sizes and player numbers, shrinking play space, limited starting equipment, and caches or chests. Items are placed randomly and players interact unpredictably, but maps—strategies for navigating them—retain a common structure between spawns.

Each battle royale game approaches these conventions differently while introducing a unique flavour to create a distinctive experience. An extremely popular battle royale game—both in terms of financial profit and player numbers—is *Fortnite* (Epic Games 2017). *Fortnite*'s battle royale game mode adheres to many of the genre's conventions, while introducing a crafting system that allows players to manipulate their environment while attempting to survive against their opponents. The sprawling, malleable environment of *Fortnite*'s map maintains its general geographical structure but introduces changes between each of the games 'seasons', which is considered one of the reasons this game has maintained popularity for so long (Feldman 2018). Similar to roguelikes, it's the tension between the structured elements of *Fortnite* that are maintained between playthroughs—or seasons—and the randomised elements that are impacted by AI systems or player choice that creates a meaningful player experience and ongoing engagement.

CONTRADICTIONS AND AMBIGUITY

Structuralism analyses texts based on the conventions and 'man-made' structures that they are designed to abide by; meanwhile, post-structuralism analyses the ways texts deviate from these expectations and break down the barriers of these structures. In addition to examining the structures outside of the text's narrative, structuralism and post-structuralism are also interested in the binary ideas, contradictions, and ambiguity present within the narrative. If you are playing a game and two ideas contained within it seem to be in opposition with each other, or the game is explicitly saying one thing but subconsciously reinforcing something else, then this is a perfect text to analyse using a post-structuralist lens. Post-structuralism also encourages the multiplicity of interpretation, allowing an audience to explore and justify multiple contradictory meanings within one text's narrative.

Games provide an opportunity for audiences to 'play' in the space between supposedly binary oppositions. *Star Wars: Knights of the Old Republic* (BioWare 2003) features an alignment system where a player's choices position the player-character as part of either the 'light side' or 'dark side' of the mysterious power known as 'the Force'. In the game, the light/dark binary is represented as a spectrum; the player is able to score between 0 and 100 on a scale that moves them between 'High dark' and 'High light', with grey areas in between. Shifting towards the light or dark side of the force imbues the player-character with special abilities and equipment, changes their appearance, and alters the way non-player–characters (NPCs) interact with them.

Despite *Knights of the Old Republic* having a numerical approach to this spectrum—where each side of the binary is represented by the lowest or highest number on a scale—this system is obfuscated for the player. The player can get a general sense of how dark or light they are based on their appearance and skills but is not granted access to the numerical value of their morality, nor are they able to see exactly the number of 'points' they gain or lose from particular actions (although a text pop-up indicates if the player has moved 'closer', 'much closer', or 'a great deal closer' to one side of the binary). Actions themselves may seem obviously 'good' or 'bad', but the game may not interpret actions the same way the player does, and this tension can create situations where a player thinks they are doing the right thing or making a completely amoral choice, but the game system decides that their choice is morally wrong.

Knights of the Old Republic features a simplified version of a morality system that is commonly more complicated in modern role-playing games (RPGs) and demonstrates the way games can encourage safe experimentation within the grey areas of binaries. By presenting players with a range of moral actions they can take and allowing them to place themselves somewhere within a spectrum, players are given opportunities for more meaningful decision-making, rather than feeling forced to act as either always good or always evil. By doing this, *Knights of the Old Republic* suggests that there are good and bad actions, but that individuals are not always at one end of the spectrum or the other, and that each person's morality can be more ambiguous. This ambiguity offers a site of analysis through a post-structuralist lens.

LESSONS AND LAMPPOSTS

Analysing The *Beginner's Guide* through a Post-Structuralist Lens

The Beginner's Guide (Everything Unlimited Ltd 2015) deliberately creates ambiguity to complicate the audience's understanding of what defines a game. In doing so, the text encourages the audience to question what is real and what signifies authenticity in media.

Despite being framed as several games developed by an individual named 'Coda', *The Beginner's Guide* is actually one cohesive game constructed by Davey Wreden. Wreden is the narrator of the game, who introduces himself in the first scene. In addition to providing the player with his name, he also talks about the game he is famous for creating—*The Stanley Parable* (Galactic Cafe 2011)—and gives the player his real email address in case they have feedback or 'interpretations' that they would like to send him. Narrator Wreden even explicitly refers to Coda as a 'real person'. By referring to his own real name, email, and background, Narrator Wreden immediately attempts to convince the player that what he is saying is authentic. When we are presented with verifiable information alongside plausible information, it is easier to believe that the latter is also true.

Blurring the line between reality and fiction is a post-structuralist approach to an assumed binary. The audience is left questioning what is real, what is fictional, and what is a half-truth. Explicitly in the game, Narrator Wreden invites us to ask what Coda's games tell us about Coda;

in doing so, Narrator Wreden implicitly asks us to consider what *The Beginner's Guide* tells us about Davey Wreden. However, the game immediately sabotages this suggestion by making it clear that it is impossible to understand a creator solely by analysing their work. In fact, this might be one of the primary purposes of the text—Narrator Wreden spends *The Beginner's Guide* examining the authorial intent of the games he makes the audience play while simultaneously revealing that he has altered these games, imposing his *own* authorial intent upon them. These contradictions force the audience to question the assumptions they make about the texts they engage with.

Ambiguity is created through what Narrator Wreden reveals and how this conflicts with the 'truths' Coda presents to us. For example, in one of the scenes, Coda begins by telling the player that the game is connected to the internet. Immediately, Narrator Wreden contradicts this, telling the player that the game is *not* connected to the internet. Similarly, Narrator Wreden tells us about the lampposts that Coda begins adding to his games as a 'destination'; but towards the climax of the narrative, Coda shares that Narrator Wreden has been adding these lampposts—and Coda would like him to stop. This ambiguity makes us question the reliability of the narrator and the version of Coda presented to us and further encourages us to question what is reality and how reality is shaped by its narrator.

Although Narrator Wreden and Coda both claim that the scenes that comprise *The Beginner's Guide* have been 'altered', it is valuable to remember that this collection of scenes is a complete game exactly as presented—'alterations' included. By using a framing narrative, Narrator Wreden creates the illusion of multiplicity. For example, in one of Coda's early games, Narrator Wreden describes the way the level 'should be' played but then alters the game to show the player a 'bug' that Coda originally created and talks about its significance. Branching narratives with multiple endings are not unusual in games; however, *The Beginner's Guide* subverts this by suggesting an interaction could have been presented in multiple ways while forcing the player to experience them linearly, in a particular order, and with Narrator Wreden's interpretations imposed on them. Further, it becomes clear that Narrator Wreden is seeking validation that his analysis is correct and, as the player cannot disagree with him at any point, *The Beginner's Guide* is inherently designed to support this outcome. Even the choice of pacing is removed from the player—game endings are 'spoiled' by Narrator Wreden before we reach them ourselves, or we are forced to move to a new scene without choice or warning.

While games are often a medium of choice, *The Beginner's Guide* is about how Narrator Wreden removes choice—both that of the player and of Coda. This creates questions for the audience regarding what defines a game and what a text needs in order to be classified as one. Narrator Wreden explicitly asks this question in one of the scenes when describing a debate he had with Coda; Narrator Wreden insists that a piece of media needs to be 'playable' to be a game. We are told a story about how Coda responds to this—he creates hundreds of games with generic box-shaped rooms that the player can walk around in without being able to do anything else. If playability is the metric by which we measure games, are these games?

This question—both in its explicit and implicit presentation in *The Beginner's Guide*—encourages the player to ask post-structuralist questions about the 'structure' of games as a medium and how a game can be deconstructed into its elements. By imposing himself on Coda's work, Narrator Wreden inadvertently shows us that games are more than a collection of elements that are combined and owned by a developer; they also require an audience. The very act of consuming a game, by necessity, requires a player to bring something of themselves to it in order to 'complete' the text. This means that each player will interpret a game differently based on the unique memories and experiences they bring to the text, and each player owns the text that they help to create—including Narrator Wreden and his interpretation of Coda's games.

A post-structuralist analysis of *The Beginner's Guide* reveals the text's multiplicity, ambiguity, and contradictions. These are deliberately designed to encourage the audience to question what defines a game and what defines reality, and how one can help inform the other. *The Beginner's Guide* shows us that texts can be a window into what is 'real' but that reality is always filtered through the perspectives of an author and an audience.

Similar to *Knights of the Old Republic*, the *Deus Ex* series allows the player to explore the ambiguous space between good and bad, heroic and villainous. The games *Deus Ex: Human Revolution* (Eidos Montréal 2011) and *Deus Ex: Mankind Divided* (Eidos Montréal 2016) each seek to create a narrative that explores prejudice by examining the relationship between humans and augmented humans. Throughout *Human Revolution*, augmented humans are presented in different ways and the player is given the opportunity to experiment within the space between good and bad extremes to help form their own opinions about whether augmented humans are 'too dangerous' to exist. This opportunity is particularly poignant because the player-character, Adam Jensen, is an augmented human, so the player is able to see first-hand the power that augmented humans can have in this gameworld.

Towards the end of *Human Revolution*, augmented humans are hacked and sent into a violent rage. As a result, there is greater prejudice against augmented humans in *Mankind Divided*. The player continues to play as

Adam Jensen and therefore should be given the opportunity to experience this prejudice first-hand; however, contradictorily, the player-character is treated as special and is allowed to focus on his privilege and skills without suffering the exploitation and marginalisation typical of augmented humans in this gameworld. When explored through a post-structuralist lens, this contradiction suggests that the text is sharing different messages explicitly and implicitly. While explicitly exploring the inescapable marginalisation and prejudicial treatment of a social group, *Human Revolution* implies that this marginalisation can be avoided with 'appropriate' behaviour and enough determination—or a greater source of privilege. Through this subtext, *Deus Ex* is suggesting that if the rest of the world considers you to be special and contributing something of value, they are more likely to treat you as human, despite the fact that all people deserve to be treated as equal regardless of their societal output.

Both structuralism and post-structuralism allow an audience to analyse games in terms of rules—both those that the text follows and those it breaks. Although these approaches may seem in competition with one another, really one is an evolution of the other, and both offer valuable opportunities to understand games based on the structures that exist outside them, that are imposed upon them, and that they are created within.

WHEN ANALYSING A GAME THROUGH A STRUCTURALIST LENS, ASK YOURSELF...

1. How does the text conform to genre?
2. How do game systems and mechanics create structure in the text? How do these structures contribute to meaning?
3. What are the binary pairings at work in the piece? Do these binaries imply a hierarchy?
4. Do words, dialogue, imagery, or allusions associated with binaries contribute to the elevation of one part of the narrative (e.g. light) over another (e.g. darkness)?

WHEN ANALYSING A GAME THROUGH A POST-STRUCTURALIST LENS, ASK YOURSELF...

1. What binary oppositions or tensions operate in the game? How are the lines blurred between binary ideas? Some examples to look for include light/dark, good/evil, old/young, linear/nonlinear, poor/rich, masculine/feminine, Western/Eastern, etc.

2. How does the text explore the space between binary ideas?
3. How does the text invite ambiguity versus certainty?
4. How does the text create the possibility of multiple meanings and interpretations?
5. How does the text allow multiple contradictory meanings to co-exist?

CHAPTER 3

Games and Class

M ARXISM IS A THEORY about class. At its core, it demands the common ownership of production, distribution, and exchange in the hope that this could lead to social power being more evenly distributed (Barry 2009: 150). Although Karl Marx (and other theorists who started the Marxist movement, like Friedrich Engels) did not make a specific statement about literature and the creation of texts, the concepts underpinning Marxism have led to a Marxist lens of textual analysis being created and applied (Barry 2009: 152).

Essentially, Marxist literary theorists suggest that a text cannot be separated from the social class in which it was written. Rather than assuming authors are struck by inspiration or genius, Marxism highlights the importance of education and opportunity, which are more easily afforded to people of a higher social class (Barry 2009: 152). This means that applying a Marxist lens to a text encourages us to focus on the aspects of class and political climate contained within that text—either explicitly or implicitly—and reflect on what these themes reveal about the world we live in.

Videogame audiences are not altogether unfamiliar with Marxism. The term is frequently used in debates about videogames, particularly regarding the relationship videogames have to diversity and representation. The games industry has had a fraught relationship with diversity (Cole & Zammit 2020), and the years of ongoing debate have led to many terms losing their meaning and significance—including Marxism. The term is now often used not to discuss and debate representations of social class; instead 'Marxist' has been co-opted as an insult for anybody with a liberal or left-leaning political alignment.

For example, when Queerly Represent Me (for which both authors are directors) conducted an audience survey in 2017 about diversity and inclusion, some participants referred to the surveyors as 'Marxist shitstains' or as being part of a 'Marxist religion'. One respondent stated that it wasn't important if character creators in videogames represented them 'because I'm not a mentally ill Marxist'. These participants may completely understand the theory of Marxism, but it wouldn't be a stretch to assume that there are some gaps in their knowledge.

The trouble is that it's easy to parrot the term 'Marxist' in incorrect and insulting contexts when political representatives and media outlets are also misusing the term. In particular, 'cultural Marxism' is an increasingly popular phrase, with a definition that has become so diluted that even the people using it don't know what it means anymore. The term was originally coined in 1973 as an extension of traditional Marxism, suggesting that it is not only capitalism that perpetuates social power, but also gender hierarchies, race relations, sexuality, and so on (Schroyer 1973). More recently, it's been picked up by conservative reactionaries as a way to claim that 'left-wing intellectuals' are 'trying to destroy the foundations of Western society' (Zappone 2017) with ideas of political correctness and privilege (Wilson 2015).

The popularity of the phrase 'cultural Marxism' has an origin story that can be traced uncomfortably close to home for the authors of this book; although first appearing in niche online forums, the term started gaining traction with a wider audience due to the work of Australian journalists and politicians. Conservative political columnist Andrew Bolt has used the phrase 'cultural Marxism' in his writing, and former Australian Labor opposition leader Mark Latham has also claimed that it is a 'powerful' movement that is 'dominating' 80% of public life (Zappone 2017). These public uses of the phrase have exposed the wider Australian public to it, encouraging its more widespread use. For radical right-wing figures, cultural Marxism has become an umbrella for ideas of postcolonialism and race studies, feminism, gender and sexuality, and social justice more broadly (Zappone 2017) and is being used to equate communism with entirely unrelated political concepts like marriage equality in the hopes that it will frighten people into voting against human rights.

Videogames as texts reveal a lot about social structures, political climates, and capitalism when viewed through a Marxist lens—but these conversations can only be valuable if shared by people with an understanding of what the theory of Marxism is actually concerned with. To this end, it's time to put aside 'Marxist' as an insult and 'cultural Marxism' as a right-wing dog whistle and, instead, consider the theory of Marxism as an analytical lens.

Existing Marxist analysis of games typically examines the medium in relation to the society in which it sits and asks questions of class and power regarding who puts labour into producing games, who has access to technology, and the ways technology now permeates our lives (Dyer-Witheford & de Peuter 2009; Kirkpatrick et al. 2016). When Marxism is used to consider the content of games, it's often focused on how designers make choices about what to include in games (Campbell 2016) rather than analysing the content itself. This is an interesting trend considering questions of power, class, and currency drive the mechanics of many games and values are being perpetuated by these decisions—either accidentally or deliberately. Multiplayer games can have a direct correlation between real-life resource ownership and in-game power, strategy games have disposable labour forces controlled by a player, and role-playing games often feature rags-to-riches storylines that comment on class.

MULTIPLAYER GAMES AND MARXISM

Multiplayer games that position players against one another competitively work as excellent exemplar texts for examining how power is distributed within class structures. In these games, in-game currency and resources act as a marker of power that can allow players to 'win' to various degrees when matched against other players. Games like *Second Life* (Linden Lab 2003) and *Star Citizen* (Cloud Imperium Games 2013) rely on in-game currency to purchase items, including ornate houses or impressive ships. These items create social hierarchies within the games—which have full economies and follow a capitalist model—and therefore lead to the development of in-game classes.

Because these open-world games don't have an end-state, being of a higher class in-game does little but allow players to have bragging rights. However, in *Star Citizen*, having access to better ships and resources means having an advantage in player-versus-player (PVP) modes, meaning 'lower class' players are limited in their ability to engage with this part of the game. This issue is amplified when the source of in-game currency is examined; players are able to buy in-game currency using real-life currency, meaning there is an immediate relationship between a person's real-life social class and their in-game social class. People with more disposable income are able to purchase more in-game resources and better ships, and therefore access parts of the game—like PVP modes—that players from lower classes are excluded from. This reinforces the way higher classes exclude lower classes in capitalist societies.

Analysing *Hearthstone*'s (Blizzard Entertainment 2014) in-game 'classes' can demonstrate how these also mirror reality. The game has been criticised for its 'free-to-play, pay-to-win' model, which suggests that anybody can download and play *Hearthstone* for free, but people with disposable real-life currency and more free time are more likely to win games because they are able to buy important in-game resources and spend time earning in-game items.

Within the 'ranked' mode of the game—where players are encouraged to compete against one another and gain a 'rank' to indicate their skill—there are particular approaches identified by players as the strongest strategies for winning. Each of these strategies requires the player to own specific cards; although players can earn these by participating in daily quests or arena challenges, the frequency with which the game is updated and competitive strategies change makes it difficult for players to participate in these strategies without paying real-life currency for cards. In this way, players with less disposable income are made to play 'catch-up' against people who are able to purchase cards and use winning strategies more reliably. This reflects the power dynamics of real-life class structures, with upper-class people being able to afford better education, healthcare, transport, and other key services that provide them with advantages, while lower classes are forced to play 'catch-up'.

EXPENDABLE LABOUR

Although many games do not feature a direct connection between real and virtual currency, they are still able to make a social comment about wealth and power when examined through a Marxist lens. The *Age of Empires* series (Ensemble Studios et al. 2019) is a well-known real-time strategy game where players lead their empire to victory by spawning villagers and armies to conquer other empires. This is a game of sheer numbers; no matter how well-prepared you are, some of your army will die in your attempts to fight your enemies, but these individuals are seen as disposable in service of the larger goal. When the population becomes too high in the later stages of a skirmish, you can literally delete villagers to make space for individuals who will 'contribute' more to the success of your empire.

This is typical of strategy games with a focus on conquering enemies. The *Total War* series (Creative Assembly & Feral Interactive 2019) highlights the disposability of labour through the combat strategies that are most effective in the game. Although these games don't explicitly tell you how to win (although they do provide tutorials and advice), the series inevitably places a value judgement on particular choices by making them more effective than others. For example, in *Rome: Total War* (The Creative Assembly 2004) an effective tactical approach involves using groups of poorly equipped soldiers recruited from poor families to attack an enemy and soften their forces, before following up with well-equipped veterans—often recruited from richer families—to finish them off. This presents the value judgement that lower-class individuals are more disposable and are not even worth giving appropriate equipment to defend themselves, while individuals from the upper class have more power within a conflict and are more worthy of protecting. This attitude reflects approaches used in actual wars and is an attempt to present realistic subject matter; however, by replicating these classist attitudes, games like *Rome: Total War* are also perpetuating them.

Guild of Dungeoneering (Gambrinous 2015) adopts a similar approach and, although it tries to lighten the themes with humour delivered via the tongue-in-cheek songs of the Bard, the disposability of adventurers for the financial gain of the guild is still uncomfortable. In this game, the player operates a guild for adventurers and must send these employees into dungeons to uncover information about the rooms; as the game progresses, the strategy of sending 'lesser' troops into the dungeons emerges, as they are more expendable than stronger, better trained troops. In this way, *Guild of Dungeoneering* exposes the way commanders view some troops as more 'valuable' than others despite each being a human life; however, unlike *Rome: Total War*, *Guild of Dungeoneering* grants the player more distance from the direct parallels between this attitude and real-life conflict because of the fantasy themes and unrealistic visual aesthetic of the game.

Marxism asks us to consider the value of the individuals who own the 'means of production' versus the individuals who are forced to sell their labour to produce a passive income for this higher class. Games that show human lives being treated unequally—with some seen as disposable cogs in a larger system while others are viewed as individually valuable—proliferate the idea that some human lives are worth more than others dependent entirely on their place within class hierarchies.

CLIMBING THE LADDER

The character development of protagonists in games—particularly role-playing games—tends to follow a 'power fantasy' trajectory, where characters gain experience, money, and abilities throughout the narrative until ultimately reaching god-like status. This common trajectory can inadvertently (or deliberately) suggest that because characters with more money and ability are 'heroic', then characters with less money or hindered ability are inherently not.

Might and Magic VII: For Blood and Honor (New World Computing 1999) follows the adventures of four protagonists controlled by the player who begin their journey by winning a scavenger hunt on a secluded island and becoming lords. Similarly, the protagonist of *The Elder Scrolls V: Skyrim* (Bethesda Game Studios 2011) begins as a prisoner and turns out to be the Last Dragonborn, the chosen hero destined to save the world. In both of these examples, the player-characters start out in a position where they lack wealth and status, and success within the narrative is based on achieving both. By linking narrative progression to the accumulation of wealth and status, games reinforce the capitalist narrative that wealth is the primary goal that individuals should strive for.

'HONESTLY, HE DOES KIND OF LOOK LIKE YOU AFTER ALL'

Analysing *Disco Elysium* through a Marxist Lens

Disco Elysium (ZA/UM 2019) explores various governmental and economic structures—both explicitly and implicitly—to reveal that each system results in similar challenges at an individual level. When institutions hold consolidated power, the power of the individual is inevitably undermined and exploited. This outcome occurs in systems where one government or individual was deliberately granted ultimate power, as well as systems that were initially designed to equitably distribute power among the masses.

Disco Elysium follows the story of a detective in the fictional city of Revachol, which is underpinned by four main ideologies: communism, fascism, moralism, and 'ultraliberalism'. Many decisions the player-character makes throughout the narrative contribute to his political alignment, which also feed into a research system called the 'thought cabinet' where the player can select various bonuses and abilities based on the alignment they have chosen. Not every 'thought' is tied to an ideology, though there is significant overlap between the two.

Although there are explicitly four ideologies in *Disco Elysium*, they go by many names. For example, the communists will use labels like 'socialists' and 'social democrats' to distance themselves from the war they lost fifty years before the events of the game. Similarly, fascists try to separate themselves from the negative connotations of that label and refer to themselves as 'traditionalists' or 'nationalists'. But no matter the name, every ideology is depicted pessimistically in a city that has been economically ravaged by revolution and occupation.

Although not explicitly named in the four pathways that the detective can pursue, the interests of capitalism are preserved by the ultraliberalist ideology, represented by the Wild Pines company and several NPCs. One ultraliberalist that the player encounters is colloquially referred to as the 'Mega Rich Light-Bending Guy' who is so rich that the laws of physics literally cease to apply when the player-character interacts with him. He claims that this is due to an 'extremely low-net-worth individual' coming into contact with an 'extremely high-net-worth individual'.

The player primarily experiences ultraliberalism through Joyce Messier, a negotiator sent by the Wild Pines company to resolve a strike that is being held by the Dockworkers' Union. The Union is a vestige of communism, and unpacking its governance immediately reveals the issues that arise when the theory of communism is applied practically. Evrart Claire—the current leader of the Union—trades leadership back and forth with his identical twin brother, Edgar, to avoid breaching the regulations of term limits. Even rules designed to enforce equity can be manipulated by institutions, as these institutions hold societal power and power leads to corruption.

The Union strike acts as the backdrop to the crime that the player-character is sent to Revachol to investigate. Essentially, a fascist mercenary—who was also sent by the Wild Pines company, to tempt participants of the strike into illegal action and potentially give leverage to negotiators—is murdered. All of these interactions between the fascists, communists, and ultraliberalists are observed by the moralists who are the current governing body of Revachol.

The Moralist International is a coalition of parties that installed themselves as suzerain of Revachol following their betrayal of the communist revolution—which ultimately led to its fall. Moralist International claim to represent 'humanism' but instead seem to care more about maintaining the status quo than they do about improving conditions through structural change.

The problem that *Disco Elysium* presents to the player is that there are seemingly no viable solutions. The remaining supporters of the overthrown communist revolution are corrupt; the moralists who took over governance are focused more on maintaining a poverty-stricken status quo than on improving conditions; and the fascists are attempting to resist through racist doctrine rather than any productive measures. Even the ultraliberalists—represented to the player through Joyce Messier—don't seem happy with the state of the world that they are attempting to maintain, but it seems that nobody is able to imagine an alternative. This reflects Western society, where many people can identify and criticise the issues with capitalism but, lacking a viable alternative, the status quo remains.

Disco Elysium suggests that all governmental and economic institutions are vulnerable to corruption, and this corruption leads to the power of individuals being exploited or destroyed. This is compounded by the suggestion that everyone is best served by looking out for their own interests—an attitude used to justify the murder that initiated the events of the game's narrative. Still, the text isn't entirely nihilistic—there is a suggestion that if individuals are able to ignore this message of egocentrism, they can reclaim their collective power by valuing and fostering community.

Although for some gamers earning in-game currency is difficult, other players end up with so much in-game currency that they can't use it all. *The Legend of Zelda: Breath of the Wild* (Nintendo 2017b), *Baldur's Gate* (BioWare & Black Isle Studios 1998), *Persona 5* (P-Studio 2017), *Destiny 2* (Bungie 2017), and the *Pokémon* series (Game Freak 2019) are just some examples of games where it becomes difficult for the player-character to run out of in-game currency, especially late-game. When a game's economy becomes unbalanced and a player is able to access any material goods they desire, it undermines the real-life challenges people face when trying to climb the ladder of social class. By incorporating these escapist ideas in otherwise capitalist societies, games blur the lines between the realistic and the fictional, and this can diminish the experiences of the real-life working class.

Currency provides power, status, and privilege; characters with more currency are able to purchase better weapons and armour, useful tools or items, or their favourite customisation options—depending on the game. In this way, the power fantasy and currency are inextricably linked. In multiplayer games, players with more currency have the additional power of being able to help—or refuse to help—other players. In massively multiplayer online role-playing games (MMORPGs) it's common for established players to aid newcomers by giving them currency and items that they might otherwise need to spend time earning. These interactions reflect the class privilege of a capitalist society; if an individual knows a wealthy person, comes from an upper-class family, or receives an inheritance, they are immediately given an advantage over individuals who enter a society without that financial aid. Sometimes these games have mechanics where currency generates *more* currency, like providing access to items with higher sell prices or investment schemes. This continues the cycle—new players with the wealthiest friends are able to become the next wealthiest players, and a class system is established.

The 'progression' systems in games are able to explicitly or implicitly reflect economic systems from society, with the common power fantasy progression idealising the capitalist idea that striving for increased wealth—and therefore power—should be each individual's ultimate goal.

WHEN ANALYSING A GAME THROUGH A MARXIST LENS, ASK YOURSELF...

1. Who has the power in the text and who doesn't? Why?
2. How do social forces shape the power relationships between groups?
3. Does the text challenge or affirm the social order it depicts?
4. How does the text reflect urban, rural, or suburban values?
5. Does the text address issues of economic exploitation?
6. How do economic conditions determine the direction of characters' lives?
7. Can a character's struggle be seen as symbolic of a larger class struggle?
8. What role does money play in the text?
9. Do any of the characters reflect types of government or economic systems, such as a dictatorship, democracy, communism, socialism, fascism, capitalism, etc.? What attitudes towards these political structures/systems are expressed in the work?
10. How does the text reflect the society in which it was created?

CHAPTER 4

Games and Women

Dᴇꜱᴘɪᴛᴇ ᴀ ꜱᴏᴄɪᴇᴛᴀʟ ꜱᴛᴇʀᴇᴏᴛʏᴘᴇ that gamers are male (Golding & van Deventer 2016), videogames did not start being designed for and marketed directly towards males until the 1980s and 1990s (Fron et al. 2007). Once videogames started to be considered 'toys', a decision (apparently) had to be made as to which binary toy aisle they would belong in. Although women had always played games, even the earliest games— including *Pong* (1972)—were often installed in gender-segregated bars, so beginning to more explicitly target game content and advertising towards boys was a logical decision (Golding & van Deventer 2016: 22). Since this divide was created, society has been positioned to consider games 'as male-oriented pursuits' (Golding & van Deventer 2016: 21–22), despite statistics revealing that nearly half of all gamers are female (IGEA 2017).

Feminism and games have a fraught relationship. Academics and critics seeking to analyse games through a feminist lens—the way they might with other texts—have been abused and harassed by a male-dominated subculture of gamers who feel that they can act as gatekeepers in the games industry because that industry has actively targeted them for years (Golding & van Deventer 2016: 28). One of the most famous examples of this is Anita Sarkeesian's 'Tropes vs. Women in Videogames' series, which was successfully crowdfunded despite a significant, wide-reaching harassment campaign towards Sarkeesian. This harassment was part of the wider GamerGate movement in 2014, which primarily targeted women in the games industry—including well-known figures like Zoë Quinn and Brianna Wu—with abuse, death and rape threats, sharing personal information online (doxxing), and intimidation tactics that forced some victims to lose their homes, jobs, and personal relationships (Golding & van Deventer 2016).

Feminism is not a direct threat to videogames and the audience that consumes them; it is a critical theory that examines texts in relation to their representation of power within a patriarchal paradigm. Put more simply: feminist analysis looks at how gender is represented in texts. Inspired by the analysis of power relationships in Marxism, feminism studies the ways in which the representation of characters are constrained by patriarchal assumptions and power structures. Feminist theory is primarily concerned with understanding and exposing areas within society that either explicitly or implicitly create inequality between women and men and, as a textual analysis lens, can be used to see whether a text challenges or perpetuates these ideas.

Definitions of feminism were initially focused on the binary separation of women and men and analysed how biological differences were used to create a power imbalance between 'females' and 'males'. As the theory developed, some feminists began to understand that believing in a universal experience of 'being female' was problematic, and that the binary separation of women and men was a false dichotomy, which has led to the birth of several variations of feminism; however, this initial revolution started a dialogue that allowed people to consider how social, cultural, and economic structures in Western society favoured men.

Historically in Western society, men have acted as the chief policy makers and leaders of social institutions—and, as such, the perspective of men have dominated social consciousness. The first wave of feminism sought to give women a voice in the decision-making process regarding the policies that affect their daily lives. Once gaining the right to vote, women began to further examine the social and cultural limitations placed on their gender. Second-wave feminism arose from this reflection and sought to provide women more control over their own sexuality and reproductive rights, as well as draw attention to male violence by citing the disproportionate cases of domestic violence and rape against women.

Third-wave feminism saw a further reclamation of the female body and a celebration of sexuality, while at the same time beginning to understand that feminist theory was not speaking for all women equally; this caused feminism to branch into even more intersectional forms including Black feminism and lesbian feminism, which destabilised the idea of the white middle-class straight cis woman's perspective being universal for all women. We are now seeing feminism expand further to acknowledge a broader spectrum of genders rather than the binary dichotomy of original feminist analysis.

Feminist theory as an approach to literature was born directly from the women's movement of the 1960s (Barry 2009). The analysis of texts was an integral part of reflecting on patriarchal structures within society and therefore textual analysis was an integral part of feminism from the beginning (Barry 2009). This makes feminism dissimilar from Marxism, which inspired a form of textual analysis years after its initial social theories were being disseminated. Feminist textual analysis has, by contrast, developed alongside the various social waves of feminism, and has concerned itself not only with the content of texts but also with the gender of individuals producing these texts. However, despite social concepts of feminism continuing to grow and embrace a broader understanding of gender, feminist criticism is still underpinned by the analysis of the binary pairings of feminine and masculine, and this chapter will be examining texts from this perspective; queer theory evolved from feminism to explore the fluidity between binary categories, and so the fluidity of gender will be explored alongside sexuality in 'Games and Queerness'.

As women became more aware of the social ideas that perpetuated female oppression and inequality, they began to reject these narratives. One way that feminists identified and vocally rejected narratives of oppression was through textual analysis, where feminist critics began to identify tropes and stereotypes. These tropes typically limit women in texts to roles that support a male character's story and emphasise traits that are seen as traditionally 'feminine'.

Feminism can also be used as a lens to identify the tropes that patriarchal society has also created for men. Men are typically depicted as either a heroic character (such as the knight in shining armour, tough guy, sexual stud, or stoic soldier) or a humorous one (such as the socially awkward nerd, effeminate man, or overweight sidekick). One character can inhabit several of these roles, blurring the line between several heroic or humorous tropes. For example, a stoic soldier might have women throwing themselves at him like a sexual stud (such as Snake from the *Metal Gear Solid* series) or a socially awkward character might also be an overweight sidekick (such as Barry Wheeler from *Alan Wake*).

Women are typically depicted in more discrete categories than men, which can make these tropes easier to identify. Archetypes like the nurturing figure, the femme fatale, and the damsel in distress each highlight different traditional social narratives of women's oppression by positioning the woman as solely a caregiver, a sexual object, or a helpless creature in need of protecting and saving.

WOMAN AS CAREGIVER

One narrative trope places women primarily in the role of caregiver. The idea that women should primarily serve as 'nurturing' figures perpetuates the idea that the purpose of women is for them to look after others, and that women have a natural propensity for being caregivers. This trope positions women as domestic and reinforces the 'ancient trope of Western writing' that assigns women the home or 'private sphere' while allowing men to own the outside world or 'public sphere' (Vickery 1993).

'Domestic' women in real life are typically housewives and stay-at-home mothers; however, mothers in videogames are uncommon. When they do appear, they are either monstrous creatures—like the giant high-heeled shoe creature in *The Binding of Isaac* (McMillen 2011) or Marguerite Baker in *Resident Evil 7: Biohazard* (Capcom 2017)—or are mostly absent. This is in stark contrast to the prominence of father figures in videogames, who often drive the plot (Bertrand 2017)—as in *Bioshock Infinite* (Irrational Games 2013) and *The Last of Us* (Naughty Dog 2013).

That said, there are still a handful of examples of mothers in games. Role-playing games like the *Pokémon* series (Game Freak 2019) and *EarthBound* (Ape & HAL Laboratory 1995) feature nameless mother characters who support their protagonist children through healing, gifts, or storing in-game currency. At face value, these characters seem like perfect examples of the nurturing figure considering they are one-dimensional women who only exist to provide a mechanical service to the player and otherwise are uninvolved in the narrative; however, closer analysis reveals they are not particularly effective caregivers considering they have encouraged their young children—between 10 and 13 years old, depending on the game and its country of release—to go on unsupervised adventures across the country. These mothers are superficially nurturing and act solely as facilitators for their (usually male) children to achieve their dreams, while remaining absent for the majority of those adventures.

Some videogame mothers nurture their children in more nuanced and present ways. Joyce in *Life is Strange* (Dontnod Entertainment 2015) is involved in her daughter (and key character) Chloe's life and is concerned for the rebellious teen throughout the story. Similarly, Candy is worried about her own rebellious teenage daughter (and protagonist), Mae, in *Night in the Woods* (Infinite Fall 2017). Both of these characters are defined by their relationship to the protagonist and their primary contribution to the plot is through the tension between their desire to nurture their daughter and their daughter's need for independence. They still fall into the 'woman as caregiver' trope but do so in a less superficial way.

The lack of mothers in videogames does not mean that the 'woman as caregiver' trope is uncommon; supportive and nurturing women still occur frequently in games despite not being literal 'mothers'. For example, in *BioShock Infinite* (Irrational Games 2013) Elizabeth is the ultimate supporter for the player-character. She spends most of the game tossing health, salts, or ammo to Booker, or else summoning useful objects for him through tears to another dimension. The items she 'finds' are not located in the environment for the player to pick up; they are seemingly conjured from thin air by Elizabeth as a way of aiding Booker, making her useful when he finds himself in a pinch.

One explanation for where Elizabeth is 'finding' these items is through those aforementioned inter-dimensional tears. Both the narrative and mechanics of the game require Elizabeth to open tears and pull objects through, but the narrative also shows that these inter-dimensional powers deplete Elizabeth's energy, causing nosebleeds and other physical symptoms. This clashes with how the mechanics work; the player can ask Elizabeth to summon freight hooks or gun automatons at will without any significant drains on Elizabeth's health, and she finds other items frequently with seemingly no impact. She will literally drop everything to aid the player upon request, such as stopping in the middle of picking a lock to summon whatever Booker asks for. Although Elizabeth has nuanced motivations and backstory in the narrative of the game, outside of cutscenes she becomes a tool for Booker to use in combat.

Elizabeth provides the player with healing, buffs, and support items, which fulfils a stereotypical female role in videogames. It's not unusual for women to play a supporting role—both as characters and players—while men are responsible for damage-per-second. Ratan et al. (2015: 19) found that women playing games are 'compelled, pressured, or otherwise directed toward playing the Support role' and that these roles are seen as 'subordinate to, and less desirable than' damage-per-second (DPS) or attack-damage-carry (ADC) roles.

Representation of characters in multiplayer videogames reinforce this stereotype. In *Overwatch* (Blizzard Entertainment 2015), players can choose between three roles: damage, tank, and support. There are more female than male characters in the support category (4:3) and less in both the damage (7:8) and tank (3:5) categories. Although this is not a large disparity, it still reinforces the assumption that more women than men will play in supporting roles while the opposite is true for damage-focused roles.

The trope of 'woman as caregiver' relegates female characters to background and supporting roles and, in turn, encourages women who play games to restrict themselves to stereotypical 'caregiving' duties—healing, buffing, and otherwise providing for their male counterparts. This has societal impacts, potentially encouraging women who play games to unconsciously perpetuate these stereotypical subservient roles in their real-life relationships.

GENDER INEQUALITY NEVER DIES

Analysing Overwatch's 'Mercy' through a Feminist Lens

Applying a feminist lens to Overwatch (Blizzard Entertainment 2015) reveals parallels between the role and function of the character 'Mercy' and the broader societal concept of inequal division of labour between men and women. Mercy belongs to the category of Overwatch heroes referred to as 'Support', meaning her mechanics primarily allow her to heal and buff damage-dealing team members to support them in securing a victory. To contextualise her supportive nature, she is depicted as a doctor and caregiver in the game through her actions and cosmetic items. Although the game's transmedia delves further into Mercy's backstory to reveal that she is also a leading researcher and scientist (Chu 2019), in-game content focuses on her being a passive caregiver.

In her role as a Support hero, Mercy has several abilities: she can heal or boost the damage of an ally, fly towards someone to reach them quickly, and resurrect fallen teammates. Although she has a pistol she can use in emergencies, her boost ability tends to help her team deal more damage than her gun can manage on its own. As a result, to effectively use Mercy's skill set, a player's accuracy with a gun is less important than their awareness of what everybody else is doing and how to best aid them in securing a victory. This 'awareness' relates to the feminist theory of division of labour.

According to research into how labour is divided between the binary genders, women perform more unpaid labour than men (Shelton 2006). Traditionally, 'women's work'—such as caring for children and the household—has facilitated the function of the formal economy by allowing men to advance their careers. Even now, as we are approaching parity between men and women in the workplace, women who are the primary earner in their household are still doing more unpaid labour than their partners (Hamid Rao 2019). This work involves a high degree of 'mental load', which describes the observation and recall required to not only perform household tasks but also notice they need to be done, plan to complete them, and delegate tasks to other members of the household if required (Ruppanner 2017). In *Overwatch*, Mercy's role is to observe the game, plan, and act accordingly; this requires a mental load that mirrors that of unpaid household labour. Her 'background' work is critical for the success of damage dealers, just as 'women's work' is critical for the success of the economy.

Mercy's cosmetic items—including her skins and voice lines—reinforce that her role is one of observation and assistance, and not of direct action. Her observant nature—and the subsequent unpaid labour she performs—is emphasised by the line she says when selected at the start of a game: 'I'll be watching over you.' When respawning, Mercy's lines include, 'Now, where am I needed?' and 'I must go where I am needed,' reiterating that her primary goals are supporting the needs of others. If she receives commendations at the end of a game, she says, 'It's nice to be appreciated,' which reflects narratives of women being underappreciated for the unpaid labour they perform in the household (Scott 2018) or 'I couldn't have done it alone!' which emphasises Mercy's role as a background actor supporting the needs of damage dealers. If Mercy happens to achieve a streak of kills with her own pistol, it's depicted as being surprising to her team with the line, 'Now this must be a surprise to you,' or to herself with the line, 'Never knew I had it in me,' reinforcing that getting kills directly is not Mercy's expected role.

Mercy's voice lines position her as a supporting character expected to work in the background to aid the achievements of the damage dealers on her team; the 'skins' or costumes she can unlock in the game links these behaviours and expectations to femininity. In particular, the Mercy skin titled 'Pink' was created as part of the Breast Cancer Research Foundation event in 2018 and was the only skin available during the event. Breast cancer—which is between 70 and 100 times more common in women than men (American Cancer Society 2020)—is inherently linked to femininity and therefore connecting Mercy to this campaign with an exclusive in-game item also links her to femininity. Moreso, because Mercy was the only woman in *Overwatch*'s hero roster to receive an item as part of this event, she is depicted as the character deemed most symbolic of womanhood—including all of the supporting behaviours and unpaid labour associated with her.

In conclusion, analysing *Overwatch*'s Mercy using a feminist lens reveals that she is presented as a symbol of womanhood. Despite transmedia depicting her as a researcher and scientist, in-game content emphasises her caregiving nature and passive approach to objectives. As such, the game associates womanhood with passivity and caregiving, as well as unpaid labour including the situational awareness and observation often associated with household chores and childcare. Ultimately, this analysis reveals that even games like *Overwatch*—which are praised for their progressive approach to representing women (Watson 2016)—can be reinforcing harmful stereotypes about what it means to be a 'woman'.

WOMAN AS SEXUAL OBJECT

'Objectification' was once a 'relatively technical term in feminist theory' (Nussbaum 1995) but has more recently become a word commonly used by reviewers and consumers when describing how women are portrayed in media. In feminist criticism, identifying situations where women are dehumanised, sexualised, or treated as objects (Nussbaum 1995) can act as a foundation for analysing a text. Videogames allow players to have more control over both characters and camera, and are therefore 'vulnerable to giving players a sense that they own the character they play' (Cross 2016). This can be particularly problematic when they are able to interact with female player-characters as though they are merely 'dolls' or 'trophies' (Cross 2016).

In *Metal Gear Solid V: The Phantom Pain* (Kojima Productions 2015), the design of non-player-character Quiet demonstrates all of these facets of objectification. Quiet is a soldier who wears a bikini top while supporting the male protagonist in combat, and remains silent for most of the game. When initial promotional images were released of Quiet's default outfit, the game's creative director responded to criticism by saying, 'Once you know the secret reason for her exposure, you will feel ashamed of your words [and] deeds' (in Scheier 2015). Both her default outfit and her inability to speak are explained in-game by the 'parasites' she is infected by; these parasites cause her to breathe through her skin using photosynthesis and will only breed (and thus further harm her) when she speaks English. However, these justifications do not hold up to scrutiny. If Quiet is unable to speak English, why doesn't she speak in a different language or spend more time communicating by writing? If Quiet needs to limit how much clothing she wears to breathe, why didn't 'The End' in *Metal Gear Solid III: Snake Eater* dress similarly—especially given that he is afflicted with the same condition?

In-game, the parasites force Quiet to be silent and scantily clad, and these parasites are analogous to the game designers who forced the same thing upon her. As she says in her final scene, 'I did not choose to be quiet'. Quiet's objectification is furthered by the optional customisations that the player can unlock for her—in particular, outfits like 'Gold Q'. This unlockable makes Quiet appear as though she is made from gold metal, turning her into a silent, moving trophy. Presenting women as trophies or as rewards for men is a trope common in texts, often tied to the 'damsel in distress' story line where a man rescues a woman and she becomes his reward. In this sense, when men are attracted to women in texts, they can become symbolic of that man's desire rather than an active character in their own right.

Lara Croft—the protagonist and player-character of the *Tomb Raider* series (Eidos Montréal et al. 2018)—has been debated by videogame critics, researchers, and players since she first appeared in the original *Tomb Raider* in 1996. In some ways, Lara is a symbol of women's empowerment: she is the leader of an action game series, was one of the first female protagonists in the medium, and has a backstory that depicts her as strong, intelligent, and decisive. But despite this, she was originally treated and talked about as a sex object and power fantasy. A 1998 New York Times article refers to Lara as a 'gun-toting, tomb-raiding sex symbol' (Barboza 1998) and describes her 'rebellious past' as an inclusion made simply to make her more attractive to her audience. Lara demonstrates that even characters who lead a franchise and appear to be active participants in their own story lines do not necessarily escape the influence of objectification.

A common technique used to disguise the objectification of women in texts is to make them more aware of their own sexual attractiveness. 'Femme fatales' are sexually desirable women who use their attractiveness to manipulate and control men for their own ends (Knight 2010) and are often depicted as negative or villainous characters. The common association between a woman's awareness of her own sexuality and villainy reflects a wider societal attitude that women should be ashamed of their sexuality (Weiss 2018).

Femme fatales are designed to be attractive to other characters within a text, but are also designed to be appreciated by a text's audience—based on the assumption that this audience is comprised of heterosexual men. The act of making a character sexually appealing to straight men—who are the assumed consumers of that text—is referred to as appealing to the 'male gaze' (Korsmeyer 2017). The male gaze is especially evident in videogames when the camera is directed up a female character's skirt or zooms in on her cleavage.

But that's not to suggest that every 'sexy' character is inherently sexualised (Cross 2016). In her essay on objectification, Nussbaum (1995) suggests that one of the primary ways we can analyse a female character to see if they are sexually empowered or a sex object is by determining whether they could be switched out for an alternative character with little or no impact on the media overall. We can do this by understanding a character's personality and then assessing their actions and poses to see if they reflect that personality or are just generically 'sexy'.

Overwatch (Blizzard Entertainment 2015) presents an interesting case study for understanding how characterisation can counteract the impacts of objectification. Two of *Overwatch*'s female heroes—Widowmaker and Tracer—wear skin-tight clothing. Widowmaker is a French sniper and her character's aesthetic leans heavily into the 'femme fatale' trope; however, the game's transmedia reveals her backstory as a ballerina turned terrorist hunter, countering the stereotypical idea of the femme fatale as villainous. Her leotard and physique are therefore references to her past career, and this justification makes Widowmaker's attire feel more like her own active choice rather than the seemingly mandatory revealing outfits of *Metal Gear Solid V*'s Quiet.

Tracer also wears skin-tight clothing, but her personality is in stark contrast to Widowmaker's. While the latter is typically intense and serious, Tracer is playful and makes frequent jokes. This is why a suggestive 'victory pose' originally released for Tracer was criticised by players (Fipps in McWhertor 2016); the issue was not that Tracer was being depicted as 'sexy' but rather that she had been given a generic, interchangeable pose rather than a pose that reflects her personality (Cross 2016). In the original pose, Tracer stands with her back to the camera and looks over her shoulder, her skin tight leggings showing her buttocks; in contrast, her new pose shows her standing on one leg in a playful 'pinup' style. In the new option, her buttocks are still visible but in a way that feels more suited to her personality. The original pose is very similar to a Widowmaker option, where the stance is much more suited to the character's femme fatale stereotype (Figures 4.1 and 4.2).

The titular character of *Bayonetta* (PlatinumGames 2009) is also a femme fatale and analysing her through a feminist lens can help determine whether her hypersexual portrayal is representative of her personality or is objectification. Returning to the idea of interchangeability, we can ask whether Bayonetta can be swapped for another character without the text losing its impact. Cross (2016) argues Bayonetta is not interchangeable: 'What makes Bayonetta special is that every inch of her style—from her clothing, her posture, her walk, her signature moves, her weapons—all say something about who she is.'

Bayonetta's sexuality is not her entire personality—it is *part* of her personality. She is not forced to wear a bikini top and remain a silent non-player-character; instead, she seems to understand and enjoy her body, as

FIGURE 4.1 Tracer's original victory pose looks generically 'sexy' (Blizzard Entertainment 2015).

FIGURE 4.2 Tracer's new victory pose tries to capture her playful personality (Blizzard Entertainment 2015).

well as the camera's attention. During her 'break dance' move, she spins her legs in the air to kick her foes before sliding towards the camera and winking at it. That said, there are some scenes in *Bayonetta* that could be seen as problematic. Generic poses in cutscenes and 'cheesy crotch shots' (Cross 2016) do little to develop Bayonetta's character, and, in these scenes, she is interchangeable with any woman of similar proportions. This observation reiterates that there isn't an inherent issue with women's sexuality being portrayed in videogames—women are only transformed into 'sex objects' when their sexuality exists for the titillation of others rather than for the expression of themselves.

WOMAN AS HELPLESS CREATURE

When women are presented to men as trophies, the woman is typically portrayed as either a sexual object or a powerless damsel. In the latter scenario, women are placed in a secondary role and are depicted as requiring the protection of a (typically male) companion.

Although Lara Croft began her life as a sex symbol—as discussed in the previous section—her role shifted in the *Tomb Raider* (Eidos Montréal et al. 2018) reboot. Although she still remained the player-character of the series, the game's executive producer, Ron Rosenberg, shared that he felt people would not 'project themselves into the character' but rather think that they're 'going on this adventure with her and trying to protect her' (in Schreier 2012). Despite the fact that Lara is the protagonist leading the adventure in *Tomb Raider*, Rosenberg specifically notes that she is being accompanied and aided by the player and therefore isn't the subject of her own story.

For Lara to be helped and protected, she must face difficult situations. Rosenberg (in Schreier 2012) outlined some of these: 'Her best friend will be kidnapped. She'll get taken prisoner by island scavengers [and] those scavengers will try to rape her.' Ultimately, the game did not include a scene with rape, with the game's brand director Karl Stewart stating that Rosenberg 'misspoke' (in Francis 2012) during this initial interview. But even if Lara doesn't experience rape or sexual assault in *Tomb Raider*, these traumas remain a common feature in the history of women in media— either as a way of demonstrating their helplessness or as the catalyst for turning them into 'strong' people.

Jessica Hammer (in wundergeek 2012) suggests that rape is commonly used in videogames because of their failure to recognise women as human beings. This limits a creator's ability to imagine the nuanced, human tragedies and problems that a woman may need to overcome, instead defining (cis) women by their genitalia—and how it's used by others. When it's not being used as shorthand for a woman's traumatic and challenging past, rape is instead turned into a symbol of the 'evil' nature of the perpetrator (Hamilton 2012; wundergeek 2012). It is used by writers as a tool to 'paint a bad guy as particularly bad and a woman as particularly vulnerable [...] without dealing with the consequences or meaning of such an act' (Hamilton 2012). In this way, the act not only makes the women involved invisible but also trivialises the reality of rape and sexual assault—crimes that are most commonly committed by individuals a woman knows and trusts (Smith 2018). This has a tangible impact on societal understandings of the prevalence and realities of sexual assault.

Although ultimately Lara's backstory in *Tomb Raider* does not include rape in the final game, she is still seen to be treated differently to male videogame protagonists for no reason other than her *femaleness*. Rosenberg (in Schreier 2012) describes how the player will want to 'root for [Lara] in a way that you might not root for a male character'. This suggests that players will want to treat her differently to protagonists of other action games—not because of her personality, history, or behaviours but because of her gender (Hamilton 2012).

Toby Gard, who worked on the original Lara back in the 1990s (in Plunkett 2012), shared a similar sentiment about players wanting to 'protect' Lara as they accompany her through the *Tomb Raider* games. However, Gard has identified that 'protecting' and 'rooting for' Lara are not the only ways players uniquely interact with her; he says players also 'loved killing her' (in Plunkett 2012). The ability to kill Lara gives players a sense of 'power' over her (Gard in Plunkett 2012), which aligns with Rosenberg's vision for the character. Rosenberg (in Schreier 2012) suggested that in this reboot Lara was going to be 'literally turned into a cornered animal', positioning her as less than human and equating her to prey.

Heavy Rain (Quantic Dream 2010) leans into the idea of the 'helpless woman' being a type of 'prey' who is continually hunted and tortured. Madison is a war correspondent who has nightmares and hallucinations due to her past experiences—although the sexually and physically violent content of these hallucinations rarely seems to reflect her real-life experiences of war. Madison is also featured in sections of the game where she is almost (or actually, depending on the ending the player achieves) killed by a taxidermist, is forced to strip for a nightclub owner, and is killed by a fire set by the game's primary antagonist. In one scene, the player—who embodies Ethan at the time—can decide whether Madison has sex with him, which removes her agency in this situation and allows the male character to determine whether she 'consents'. *Heavy Rain* does not treat Madison as a human being, but rather as a powerless 'toy' for the audience to play with.

These examples show two extremes of how narratives represent the 'helpless woman' archetype: as a character for the player to protect or as a creature for the player to harm. An additional iteration of the archetype places the helpless woman off-screen for most or all of the narrative, with the promise of her existence acting as a motivator for the protagonist's 'quest'. This subcategory—referred to as the 'damsel in distress' trope—positions the woman as a symbol that the protagonist must seek out and rescue from an antagonist or circumstance. Upon completing their quest, the protagonist—and player—is often 'given' the woman as a prize, removing the woman's agency in making choices for the direction of her own life.

Double Dragon (Technōs Japan 1987) is an early game that features this trope. It was originally released as a multiplayer arcade game featuring two main characters, the twins Billy Lee and Jimmy Lee. These two brothers are both enamored with a dojo student named Marian; after defeating several waves of Black Warriors' gang members, Jimmy and Billy—and, as such, the two players—battle one another, and the winner claims Marian as a prize. When the game was ported to consoles that only offered single-player options, the narrative was modified so Jimmy Lee was the leader of the gang and kidnapped Billy's girlfriend, Marian, ensuring that the two brothers could still fight over the damsel in distress.

Another early example of the 'damsel in distress' can be found in *Donkey Kong* (Nintendo 1981). The game has a simple story: Jumpman is attempting to rescue 'Lady' from the eponymous Donkey Kong. Even though neither human character is named, Jumpman has an action attached to his title—'Jump'—which positions the male as an active force, while the female is defined by her gender and plays a passive role in the story. Later, 'Lady' was renamed Pauline and has played minor roles in the *Donkey Kong* and *Mario* series. While she has a 'major' role as a mayor in *Super Mario Odyssey* (Nintendo 2017a), Pauline's first appearance as a playable character came in 2018, where she debuted as an option in *Mario Tennis Aces* (Camelot Software Planning 2018). Similarly, the predominant narrative for the *Super Mario* series is Princess Toadstool's abduction and subsequent need to be rescued by Mario—and the player.

In all three of the archetypes explored in this chapter—woman as caregiver, sexual object, and helpless creature—a woman is depicted in terms of her relationship to the (typically male) protagonist rather than as their own character. Applying a feminist lens to texts allows us to identify situations where characters are present only to support, motivate, or titillate other characters and unpack the gendered norms that underpin these representations.

WHEN ANALYSING A GAME THROUGH A FEMINIST LENS, ASK YOURSELF...

1. How are men and women represented? Are they depicted in distinctly different ways?
2. What relationships can be identified between men and women in the text? Are these relationships a source of conflict?
3. What is the default power dynamic between masculinity and femininity in the text?
4. Does the game challenge or affirm traditional representations of masculinity and femininity?
5. How are masculine and feminine ideas portrayed in the game? Are these considered to be binary ideas and/or connected to gender?
6. How are characters who subvert traditionally masculine or feminine presentations perceived by others?
7. Are women in the game present only to support, motivate, or titillate the protagonist (and player) or are they nuanced, standalone characters?
8. What behavioural expectations are imposed on characters and what effect do these expectations have?
9. What marital expectations are imposed on characters and what effect do these expectations have?
10. How does the society depicted in the game relate to the patriarchal structures of our society? Compare them economically, politically, socially, and psychologically.

CHAPTER 5

Games and Queerness

CRITICAL ANALYSIS OF QUEERNESS in texts has multiple origins. 'Lesbian feminism' emerged in the 1980s as a way of highlighting that lesbian women have different social needs and are fighting for different rights than the white straight woman that feminist theory originally treated as the default (Barry 2009). In response, 'queer theory' emerged in the 1990s as a way of looking at both lesbian and gay representations rather than focusing solely on lesbians through the lens of feminism (Barry 2009).

Neither of these two approaches is yet to adequately and explicitly dedicate itself as studying the diverse sexualities and genders that comprise the queer community beyond lesbians and gay men. The area of queerness in games is a burgeoning field of study, with many papers and books being published on the topic in recent years (Ruberg & Shaw 2017), but the majority of in-game representation and supporting research still focuses on these same representations of lesbians and gay men.

This chapter will be reflecting on the analytical approaches of lesbian feminism and queer theory, while also exploring representations of people attracted to multiple genders, people who do not experience sexual attraction, and people who have trans or nonbinary genders. This broader and more inclusive approach can be referred to as 'queer criticism' and involves understanding common tropes and stereotypes associated with the queer community, identifying them within games, and interpreting what they reveal about society's perception of queer people. Although analysing texts in this way has less of a theoretical framework underpinning it than the approaches we have considered thus far, it mirrors aspects of these lenses and creates a space for reflecting on the representations of other marginalised identities.

Queer criticism is derived from feminist textual analysis, which positions masculine and feminine traits as binary opposites to one another. Feminist analysis can be used to examine how a text treats these characteristics; for example, this lens encourages us to ask whether feminine traits are typically assigned to women in a text, if traditional understandings of gender are being subverted, or if binary ideas of gender are being blurred. Similar questions can be asked in queer criticism to understand how traditionally masculine and feminine traits are used to 'code' queer characters and themes in games, as well as how diverse genders are represented.

MASCULINITY, FEMININITY, AND SEXUALITY

One common trope in the representations of gay men and lesbian women is to flip traditionally masculine and feminine characteristics, depicting gay men and lesbians as having stereotypical traits of the opposite binary gender. There are many examples of feminine gay men in games, with some early games relying on their stereotypical 'flamboyance' as the sole indicator suggesting their sexuality. This flamboyance is portrayed through a male character's enthusiastic and often high-pitched voice, stylish clothing choices, and exaggerated physical movements.

More recently, sexuality and same-sex relationships have started to be made more explicit in games, meaning that players don't have to make assumptions about a character's sexuality based only on their appearance or mannerisms; however, even gay characters who are explicit about their same-sex attraction are often still represented in this stereotypical way. In *Red Dead Redemption 2* (Rockstar Studios 2018), Quique Montemayor is depicted with flamboyant mannerisms as shorthand for communicating his sexuality. This characterisation provides context for Quique's flirtations with Vincente de Santa and encourages the player to view their interactions as sexual rather than platonic and humorous. Similarly, Antoine in *My Time at Portia* (Pathea Games 2019) tells the player how much he likes and cares about Dr. Xu, a male doctor who runs a clinic on the island. This fixation could be seen as admiration rather than romantic attraction; however, the game depicts Antoine with pink hair, an obsession with skin care, and 'sashaying' walk animations, encouraging the player to interpret him as gay by associating him with stereotypically feminine colours, priorities, and mannerisms.

Skin care and makeup are both treated as traditionally feminine routines in Western society, and so depicting male characters as being interested in these products is one of the tools used in texts when trying to imply that they are gay. In *Persona 2: Innocent Sin* (Atlus 2011), Kurosu Jun's original character art shows him wearing lipstick, and the game features in-game dialogue where Lisa laments that Kurosu looks better in makeup than she does. In *Resonance of Fate* (tri-Ace 2010), makeup is similarly used to depict the bartender of Le Chit-Chat Noir as gay.

Another way games attempt to convey a male character's sexuality through his femininity is with his voice and dialogue. In the *Valkyria Chronicles* (Sega 2008), Jann Walker often uses terms of endearment in his dialogue like 'honey' and 'sweetie'; these affectionate terms convey emotion and connection, which are typically associated with femininity (in contrast with the logic and stoicism of masculinity). In *Grand Theft Auto IV* (Rockstar North 2008), Bernie Crane is even assigned a female voice artist, and his character uses the generic female scream sound when he is injured in the game.

When gay men in games are depicted as having stereotypically feminine traits, these are often superficial and based on the character's physicality or appearance. However, when women are depicted as 'masculine' and therefore implied to be lesbians, their masculinity is often portrayed instead through their personality, career choices, and hobbies. For example, *Horizon Zero Dawn* (Guerrilla Games 2017) features Petra, a woman who works with machines and cannons; similarly, *Borderlands: The Pre-Sequel* (2K Australia & Gearbox Software 2014) introduces Janey, a junk dealer. Working with their hands on machinery and junk is not a traditionally feminine career, and leads to both characters being shown in practical clothing and with dirty skin. However, while feminine men are often depicted in a way that makes them seem comedic, masculine women are instead presented in a way that heterosexual men are still likely to find attractive. This practical clothing—often coupled with short hair—remains paired with thin, curvy body shapes and soft, feminine facial features.

'Butch' women with masculine physiques—including larger builds, muscle mass, and angled features—are far less common in games. Where they are present, they are assumed by audiences to be lesbians even if this remains unconfirmed, such as in the case of Zarya from *Overwatch* (Blizzard Entertainment 2015). Of *Overwatch*'s cast of characters, one has been confirmed to be a lesbian but rather than the stereotypically 'butch' woman, it was Tracer who was assigned this identity. Tracer—an ex-pilot with a short pixie haircut—more closely aligns to the trope of making lesbian characters masculine only in ways that ensure they remain attractive to the heterosexual male gaze.

Using stereotypically feminine traits to depict gay men as comedic associates femininity with humour, while masculine traits held by attractive women are seen as improvements. This not only reinforces problematic assumptions about sexuality but also creates a harmful narrative around whether having masculine or feminine traits is inherently positive or negative.

CROSS-DRESSING AND RESPECT

Cross-dressing is one technique used as shorthand to depict an individual's sexuality, such as when a man is shown as wearing makeup to suggest that he is gay (as covered in the previous section). However, cross-dressing can serve purposes unrelated to sexuality in games as well, despite being a practice commonly associated with 'queerness'. A common trend is for protagonists to use cross-dressing as a way to sneak into areas or fool other characters.

In *Final Fantasy VII* (Square 1997), Cloud cross-dresses to sneak into the headquarters of a slumlord. Similarly, in *The Legend of Zelda: Breath of the Wild* (Nintendo 2017b), Link has to dress as a woman to enter Gerudo Town, a place where only women are permitted. Both of these examples depict a male protagonist cross-dressing as a strategy to sneak into an area necessary to further their quest. Despite this similarity, there is an integral difference between these representations: Cloud is attempting to fool a male slumlord who wields power while Link uses cross-dressing to deceive women into letting him enter a women's space. In patriarchal society, men hold more social and structural power than women, and women's spaces are created as areas of safety and relief; implying that deceiving women to enter one of these spaces is acceptable or even humorous undermines the necessity of these spaces within society and turns them into a joke.

The trend of men dressing as women in texts for the sole purpose of sneaking into women's spaces perpetuates an unfounded fear that cis men will use policies designed to protect trans people to access women's spaces and prey on their users. There is no evidence that these crimes increase with the implementation of policies that guarantee trans people the right to use spaces suited to their gender (Marza 2014); however, texts reinforcing this fear can lead to more widespread resistance to trans rights even if it is not founded in fact.

When men cross-dress as women in games, they are often depicted in a humorous way, losing the respect of other characters or the player; in contrast, when women cross-dress as men, they often do so to *gain* respect. In *Final Fantasy V*, Faris works as a pirate captain and cross-dresses as a man to maintain the respect of her crew. In *Persona 4* (Atlus 2008), Naoto cross-dresses as a man to be taken seriously as a detective. In *The King of Fighters* (SNK et al. 2016), King cross-dresses to become a respected fighter and to be permitted in the Muay Thai ring.

In a patriarchal social structure, being a man is more respected than being a woman. This explains why a woman can disguise herself as a man to gain more respect, while men in feminine clothing are found entertaining by other characters or the audience. Contrasting these representations using a feminist lens (as per Chapter 4) reveals the inequality between how each binary gender is seen within society; however, applying a queer theory lens to this representation allows us to instead examine how society views lesbians and gay men specifically. As we have already explored, gay men are often depicted as feminine and lesbian women as masculine as a shorthand for expressing their sexuality to an audience. It follows then that gay men are seen as less respected than lesbian women due to their association with femininity, a less respected set of traits within patriarchal society. This aligns with studies which have found that lesbian women are more accepted than gay men in social structures including governments, sports teams, and popular media (Fitzsimons 2020).

BEYOND THE BINARY

Despite its historical focus on gay and lesbian identities, 'queer theory' also suggests that researchers should look for instances of binaries being dissolved and fluidity being embraced within texts (Barry 2009). This post-structuralist approach encourages us to expand how we apply queer theory to texts, using it to identify and explore representations of the broader range of sexualities and genders within the queer community.

Increasingly, our understanding of gender objects to the idea of a binary, instead opting to consider gender as a spectrum or multiplicity, with blurred boundaries that an individual might move between fluidly (Linstead & Brewis 2004; Linstead & Pullen 2006). We can use queer theory to identify situations where these gender binaries are dissolved, as well as analyse the ways a fictional world interacts with gender-diverse characters and reflect on what these representations reveal about our society.

Although still uncommon, explicitly transgender characters are gradually being introduced in more videogames. This includes characters who identify as a binary gender as well as characters who identify as genders outside the binary or have a fluid gender identity. In some instances, these characters are easy to identify, with developers flagging—literally—their existence within a game. In *Borderlands 3* (Gearbox Software 2019), the character 'Fl4k' wears a pin on their jacket with the nonbinary flag colours, featuring a line crossing through 0s and 1s—a reference to their identity as a nonbinary robot. In the game, Fl4k's gender is irrelevant to how this player-character functions mechanically, making this a simple way for *Borderlands* developers to incorporate greater diversity into the game with few additional requirements.

Instead of using a literal flag to denote a character's identity, character gender can be explored through dialogue; in these instances, even more work needs to be done to ensure a text is representing characters authentically and appropriately. One challenge developers face in crafting these representations is how to make it clear that a character is trans, nonbinary, or gender fluid without them oversharing information about themselves in an unrealistic way. For example, in *Pokémon X/Y* (Game Freak 2013), a Beauty Trainer (an all-female group of NPCs) in the Battle Maison tells the player-character that they used to be a Black Belt (an all-male group of NPCs). In the English translation, the Beauty Trainer refers to this as 'quite the transformation' while the original Japanese dialogue references the power of medical science (Mandelin 2014). This interaction uses dialogue to imply that the character is trans.

Similar to Fl4k in *Borderlands 3*, the Beauty Trainer's gender is irrelevant to how they play mechanically and therefore making this character trans is an easy way to incorporate gender diversity into *Pokémon X/Y* while having limited impact on the game itself and how it is developed. However, the Beauty Trainer differs because of how her gender is revealed to the player; instead of a pride pin—a common accessory worn by members of the queer community—the Beauty Trainer immediately tells the player-character about her 'transformation' with no prompting. This interaction is jarring and inauthentic; most people don't introduce themselves to strangers by enthusiastically revealing personal information about themselves. This representation reveals the ignorance that society still has towards trans people and the ways they might authentically interact with strangers on the topic of their gender.

Similarly, in *Mass Effect: Andromeda* (BioWare 2017b), a scene where Hainly Abrams introduces herself had to be removed after her discussion of gender was found to be inappropriate and offensive to the trans community. In this scene, Hainly revealed to the player-character that she is a trans woman when they were practically strangers and then proceeded to reveal her 'deadname'—the name she used before she transitioned. As Laura Kate Dale (2017) states in her editorial on the topic, 'Having their dead name brought up isn't a problem for some trans people. For many, myself included, it is. Hearing my pre-transition name is an emotional gut punch that reminds me of how bad I felt during that part of my life'. Hainly immediately revealing a detail that is so emotional for many trans people made her representation inauthentic, and this inauthenticity can perpetuate ignorance among players who may think—and continue thinking—that talking about topics like deadnames is acceptable.

Ignorance is a common thread that can be identified in representations of transgender, nonbinary, and gender fluid characters. While in some cases, this ignorance is an accidental expression of the developers' own, in other cases it is deliberately expressed in-game by a player-character as a cipher for the player.

In an earlier BioWare game, *Dragon Age: Inquisition* (BioWare 2014), the player-character has the opportunity to select from some ignorant questions during a conversation with Krem. At this point in the game, the player-character has had several interactions with Krem already and the topic of his gender arises in a relatively natural way—via a joke between Krem and another NPC, Iron Bull. This representation can be interpreted as a reflection of the lack of understanding still common in wider society and as providing the player with an educational opportunity; however, this representation has also received some criticism from trans people as the player-character is able to ask personal questions about Krem's physical attributes without being rebuffed. This can incorrectly teach players that it is acceptable to ask a trans person these questions. Representations that involve a character revealing their deadname or a protagonist asking a trans character about their physical attributes without consequences reveal underlying truths about the current overarching societal understanding of how trans people can—and should—be treated.

In *The Witcher 3: Wild Hunt* (CD Projekt Red 2015), Geralt encounters a character named Elihal while searching for one of Dandelion's girlfriends.

Elihal originally appears wearing masculine clothing and speaking with a low voice but, when Geralt asks about Dandelion, Elihal walks into an adjoining room and returns in feminine clothing and makeup. When Geralt says, 'So you're...' Elihal responds simply with, 'Elihal'. Geralt's additional questions are somewhat more subtle than those of *Dragon Age: Inquisition*'s player-character and Elihal frequently jumps in to offer information before being asked for it, mostly focused on the nature of their relationship with Dandelion. This representation shows that a player-character can be ignorant and unsure how to respond to gender diversity in-game, while still allowing a gender-diverse character to be an authentic portrayal and simultaneously avoiding being offensive to trans people in the text's audience. In doing so, this representation also models ways that ignorant people in society can be confused by an unfamiliar situation but still navigate conversations on the topic while being less likely to sound insensitive or offensive.

Not all representations of gender diversity are explicitly included in dialogue exchanges—or in the game at all. Some characters are treated as gender-neutral in a source text without anything in-game referring to their gender explicitly; their gender identity is then confirmed externally through accompanying media or developer statements—or isn't confirmed at all. For example, in *Pokémon Go* (Niantic 2016) one of the team leaders—Blanche—is referred to as 'they' in a blog post designed to be read as an update log written by Professor Willow, the in-game professor (Niantic 2019), but their gender identity has not been confirmed, nor has it been made explicit within the game itself. Similarly, *Apex Legends'* (Respawn Entertainment 2019) Bloodhound is referred to with they/them pronouns in their official EA biography (EA 2020) but their gender is not confirmed or referred to within the game.

When examined through a queer criticism lens, this incidental representation could be considered an acknowledgement that people with diverse genders exist and therefore should be incorporated in games even when an individual's gender doesn't matter to—or even get mentioned in—the content of a game. This allows a gameworld to become more nuanced and true to life. However, an alternative argument can be made: by including gender diversity only in supplementary content, it's easier for companies to appease LGBTQ+ players without enraging—and potentially losing—their conservative audience.

Celeste (Matt Makes Games 2018) features a scene in Chapter 9 where the protagonist, Madeline, is chatting on her computer with tiny gay pride and trans pride flags sitting on her desk. This seems like a nod towards Madeline's sexuality and gender—similar to the nonbinary pin on Fl4k's jacket—but the developers have not commented on whether or not Madeline is trans (Dale 2019). Although the representation within the game itself suggests that Madeline is trans and this interpretation can exist without authorial intent or input, this representation has implications for a game audience. Dale (2019) notes that although implicit representation is a good way of showing that being queer is 'no big deal', not confirming this representation 'empowers those who would rather not face the fact they might have played as a trans person in a game they like'. This can result in situations like 'moderators on the Celeste Wiki [taking a] stance against Madeline being a trans character' (Dale 2019), despite the interpretation that Madeline is trans being a valid analysis of the text. This disempowers trans audiences, perpetuates societal norms, and demonstrates the need for multifaceted textual analysis of games.

Games that feature ambiguous depictions of gender provide us with opportunities to analyse these representations and identify the multiplicities; however, when the wider games community is not approaching games from the same analytical standpoint, interpretations become invalidated—and identities along with them.

ERASURE

The erasure of identities is not evident only in the games community—it is also present within texts themselves. When approaching a text using queer criticism, you can look at the gaps and spaces within that text rather than the representations of characters and themes that are featured. Erasure of queer identities—particularly queer identities that are even marginalised within the queer community, like bisexual, pansexual, asexual, and nonbinary identities (Walker 2016)—is a societal issue that is reflected within texts.

In some instances, erasure of queer identities in games is deliberate and explicit. When *RimWorld* (Ludeon Studios 2018) was first released, in-game code was discovered that dictated the way 'pawns' interacted with each other and formed relationships. This code created rules that the AI followed as it made decisions, including how each pawn decided who they found attractive. These rules were applied differently to male and female pawns, with each finding different ages and genders attractive. For example, male pawns were always either gay or straight, while female pawns were either gay or bisexual (Lo 2016).

These rules were changed in subsequent updates of the game but examining this original text suggests certain assumptions about how different (binary) genders experience sexuality and sexual attraction. The conscious choice to include code that makes heterosexual women and bisexual men impossible within *RimWorld* actively erases these identities from the game. This reflects society's acceptance of some sexualities and genders within the queer community over others, relating back to our previous examination of how society responds to lesbians versus gay men (Fitzsimons 2020).

However, there are other ways erasure of queer identities can manifest in games. It can be argued that explicit representations of bisexuality, pansexuality, and other multiple-gender-attracted people are erased from games that use 'playersexuality' as a mechanic. 'Playersexuality' is a term used to describe games where romanceable NPCs are attracted to the player-character regardless of their gender, rather than having an identity and romantic history that exists outside of the character's feelings towards the player. It is a mechanic that is particularly common in open-world games that emphasise player freedom (Cole 2017), which seek to allow players to go wherever they like, do whatever they want, and date whomever they prefer. For example, in *The Elder Scrolls V: Skyrim* (Bethesda Game Studios 2011), there are 30 women and 35 men that all player-characters can marry, regardless of gender. Each of these characters require the player to complete a task to 'romance' them, from succeeding in a quest, to chopping wood or giving them grapes. Despite this large number of romanceable character options, each of these characters has a limited individual identity—including no relationship history in most cases—meaning that they are attracted exclusively to the player rather than to particular personalities, appearances, or genders. In addition, despite the fact that each of these romanceable characters are willing to date player-characters of the same gender, there are almost no other same-sex relationships in the gameworld of *Skyrim*.

The fact that 65 characters can be interested in a same-sex relationship within *Skyrim* but only with the player is indicative of the fact that these characters are not bisexual, pansexual, or some other form of plurisexual—they are *playersexual*. They are interested in the player no matter who they are and they are interested in nobody else. By creating the option for players to experience same-sex relationships, players are able to introduce queerness into the game if they choose to but can still have limited exposure to same-sex couples if they'd prefer a heterosexual experience. Plurisexual people are always plurisexual, no matter who they are dating, and hiding the sexuality of romanceable characters unless it serves the player contributes to the erasure of these identities.

PLAYERSEXUALITY IN PELICAN TOWN
Analysing *Stardew Valley* Using Queer Criticism

Stardew Valley (ConcernedApe 2016) is a simulation game where the player-character moves to a farm in Pelican Town and tends crops, explores mines, and forms relationships with townsfolk. There are twelve romanceable characters in *Stardew Valley*—six men and six women—and each can be dated by any player-character, regardless of gender. Each of these characters has no sense of self-identity, have limited heteronormative relationship histories, and exist within a heteronormative gameworld.

Each romanceable NPC in *Stardew Valley* has items that they like and dislike, including favourite items that they become particularly excited about. The player-character is able to give these items as gifts, which is the easiest way to raise their 'friendship score' with the NPC. Although there are some other methods of raising friendship scores—such as having conversations or making certain choices in cutscenes—regular gift-giving is the most effective method for improving the player-character's relationship with anybody else on the island.

To date an NPC, the player-character's friendship score with that character needs to become high enough. Once the score is maxed out, it's possible to propose marriage to the NPC. This mechanic suggests that the progression from stranger to friend to spouse is a linear one, which is reinforced by your spouse becoming jealous if you give gifts to anybody else and increase your friendship score with them. This contrasts with the diverse and interesting relationships *Stardew Valley* tries to create between NPCs, which includes siblings, co-workers, and platonic relationships that cross gender boundaries. Some of the single characters in town are friends with each other and can be seen socialising together at different times in their schedules, so why does the game attempt to shame the player-character for forming friendships with single characters and being generous towards these friends once they are married to somebody else?

In addition to platonic and familial relationships, there are also a number of existing romantic couples in Pelican Town including Evelyn and George (an older married couple), Jodi and Kent (with Kent only returning home in the second in-game year after serving in the army), and Demetrius and Robin (another married couple with children). It is also suggested that Mayor Lewis is seeing Marnie when the player is tasked with locating his pants, which can be found in Marnie's bedroom. Despite these interesting romantic relationships at different stages throughout Pelican Town, there are no same-sex relationships in the game.

This is particularly interesting when it is considered that twelve different characters in Pelican Town are single and potentially interested in a same-sex relationship with the player-character if the player-character initiates one. Why is there no evidence of any of these eligible villagers ever dating each other? The implication that each of them has eyes only for the player and has no romantic history reinforces that these characters are not plurisexual but are simply *playersexual*. Although each NPC has likes and dislikes towards items and gifts, they have no preferences towards who they date and the appearance, personality, or gender of the player-character is irrelevant to their desire to be married to them provided they have been given enough presents. By limiting a sense of personal history for each character—especially in regard to relationships—the game centres sexuality around the player and erases the sexuality of NPCs.

The lack of same-sex relationships—either present or historical—in Pelican Town puts pressure on the player if they would like their character to embark on a same-sex relationship. Mirroring the uncertainty of coming out in real life, there is no indication as to how a potential same-sex partner might respond to the suggestion of dating or how the rest of Pelican Town might react. Is it safe to be in a same-sex relationship in Pelican Town and the surrounding locales of Stardew Valley?

If the player-character does engage in a same-sex relationship, the player must then field awkward questions and interactions with NPCs who are accustomed to a heteronormative town. This includes George making uncomfortable comments about you having a same-sex partner and Mayor Lewis hesitating with how to announce you both after officiating your wedding. This unfamiliarity seems to be confined to the locations explored in *Stardew Valley* and is not reflected within the structures that govern the gameworld; a same-sex couple is able to adopt a baby as easily as an opposite-sex couple is able to conceive one, suggesting same-sex relationships are legally acknowledged and respected in this world.

Stardew Valley allows the player-character to date any eligible NPCs in Pelican Town, regardless of gender, as a way to suggest that all sexualities are accepted in this setting; however, by making the town heteronormative in its other romantic relationships, the game demands that queer player-characters must be torchbearers for marriage equality, including dealing with curious questions and awkward interactions with other NPCs.

Playersexuality relates to the larger issue of texts relying on internal and imagined storylines created by the player to include queer representations. By hinting at potentially diverse sexualities and genders, games are able to inspire queer audiences to develop 'headcanons', which are unconfirmed imagined stories that *could* be true.

Applying queer criticism to a text can involve looking at opportunities for audiences to create queer headcanons. In *Dragon Age: Inquisition* (BioWare 2014), 'Cole' is an example of a character whose representation led to headcanons in the game's audience. Cole is a spirit who never explicitly refers to himself as asexual but, during a conversation with Solas, he reveals that he doesn't feel attraction; this reference allowed the game's asexual audience to establish a headcanon that Cole's sexuality was a representation of their identity. This was undermined in the *Trespasser* downloadable content, where the player is given the opportunity to help Cole become human. If the player assists him, Cole forms a relationship with a woman and explains this by saying, 'Well, I am human now'. This representation implies that the reason Cole did not feel attraction previously was due to him being a spirit and not a human, and therefore that all humans feel sexual attraction. Not only does this conflict with the headcanon audiences had established and remove the possibility of Cole's asexuality, but this representation also suggests that asexual people are somehow less human than allosexual people. This not only erases asexuality from the text but also suggests it does not exist in society.

In addition to erasing individuals and their identities from texts, queer criticism can also be applied to games to reveal instances of queer communities being erased. When a queer character is present within a game, it's unusual for any other queer characters to be included alongside them (Shaw et al. 2019). When more than one queer character is included together, they are typically romantic partners (Shaw et al. 2019). A common refrain by audiences who are hesitant about increasing diversity in games is that it is unrealistic to have large groups of queer characters in one game or scene (Queerly Represent Me 2017)—especially considering only 5%–10% of the population self-identifies as LGBTQ+ (The Williams Institute 2019). However, if we always aim to ensure that there are nine (or nineteen) straight cisgender people for every one queer person in a text, we are removing the context of how queer individuals interact with each other in reality.

The term 'LGBTQ+ community' or a similar variation has become extremely common but can mean different things depending on who is using it (Formby 2017). It can be a generic term that is used as a synonym for 'people' or 'population', a physical space where queer people gather, or an abstract space where queer people can find 'support or similarity' (Formby 2017). Regardless of the definition used, the existence of an LGBTQ+ community suggests that there are spaces where queer people congregate, situations where queer people interact, and contexts where queer people are otherwise considered collectively. This means it is not unrealistic to depict multiple LGBTQ+ people interacting within the same space—physical or virtual—and games that only represent queer people as individuals or pairs are erasing these communities.

2064: Read Only Memories (MidBoss 2015) is one game that specifically seeks to represent the queer community. Within the physical space of the Stardust nightclub, individuals of assorted sexualities and genders congregate and will have conversations with the player-character. This is one of few examples of multiple queer characters sharing a space within a game, and it's within a game that was specifically developed to be 'queer-inclusive' (Ligman 2013). In the few games where queer community is explored, it is often at a superficial level and most commonly revolves around the physical space of a 'gay bar' (Shaw 2020). These representations of queer community suggest that queer people rarely congregate and, when they do, they primarily meet one another in bars. This has the consequence of associating queerness with extroverted behaviour and alcohol and stereotypes queer people as having a specific set of personality traits rather than reflecting the reality that queer people—and communities—are diverse. It also associates queerness with adulthood, erasing queer children and teenagers, and failing to acknowledge their need for a community to provide them with 'support and similarity' as they establish their identities.

Queer criticism allows us to examine explicit representations of queerness in games, but also encourages us to understand the 'queerness' that can be found in subverted binaries, gender fluidity, gaps and silences, and audience headcanons.

WHEN ANALYSING A GAME USING QUEER CRITICISM, ASK YOURSELF...

1. How is queer content treated within the text's thematic content or character portrayals?
2. What does the text contribute to our knowledge of queer, gay, or lesbian experiences and history, including media history?
3. What does the text reveal about society's social, political, or psychological discrimination of diverse sexualities and genders?
4. In what ways are characters represented as 'masculine' or 'feminine'? How do these representations relate to their perceived sexuality?
5. How does the text represent relationships? Who is romantically interested in whom and what does this reveal about the game-world's attitudes towards diverse sexualities?
6. What opportunities for queer representation are not explored in the text?
7. How is queer community explored or erased in the text? Are there examples of physical or abstract communities? What are their purposes?

CHAPTER 6

Games and Race

Postcolonial theory suggests that all texts make a social comment about power relationships; however, unlike the theories in the previous chapters that have been concerned with class, gender, and sexuality, postcolonial theory examines texts for their representations of race (Barry 2009: 186). This theory explicitly challenges liberal humanism's claim that all texts can convey a universal human experience and is instead founded on the idea that texts are interpreted differently depending on the identity of the individual. Postcolonial theorists proclaim that people of different races have different life experiences, and these are reflected in both the creation and consumption of texts.

One of the main pillars of postcolonial criticism is that non-white characters are treated as an 'Other' in texts (Barry 2009). To understand this, you first need to understand what we mean by 'white' in this context. 'Whiteness' is not about the literal colour of a person's skin, but rather the cultural and political climate of a particular time period; 'whiteness' is not a static or consistent category (Twine & Gallagher 2008) and excludes or includes different groups in different time periods. For example, 'whiteness'—and the privilege of being part of the socially accepted race—has historically excluded Italians, Greeks, the Irish, or Jews (Jacobson 1999; Guglielmo 2000) due to political relationships and views on immigration.

This perspective of 'whiteness' is America-centric and based on immigration trends within the US during the 19th and 20th centuries. Discussions of race—and therefore of colonial and postcolonial ideas— were originally oriented around British views, but have shifted from

British ideals to American ones as the British Empire fell and the US began to establish itself as an 'empire' in its own right (Höglund 2008). One way the influence of these 'empires' can be seen is through the way media representations of the 'Other' are used to legitimise foreign policy.

For example, the British Empire created negative representations of the East in their media to make 'British colonial policy both possible and agreeable to the British and European public' (Höglund 2008). These representations are referred to as 'orientalism', which is a concept founded by Edward Said in *Orientalism* (1978). Historically, the term 'orientalism' refers to the ways the media (including journalism, literature, political public relations, and even academia) represented Eastern regions to legitimise—and 'enable' (Höglund 2008)—British expansion over the East.

Similarly, 'orientalism' can be seen in American media where representations are used to perpetuate stereotypes, spread fear, and make citizens agreeable to US foreign policy. For example, American media during the Cold War typically positioned Soviets as a stereotypical enemy, and this can be seen reflected in games like the *Command & Conquer: Red Alert* series (Electronic Arts & Westwood 2009), which presents itself as a 'historical' game with realistic weapons and vehicles; however, the game allows American armies to access 1980s tanks alongside Soviet 1940s aircrafts (Kukulak 2018). More recently, similar orientalism is also evident in media representations of the Middle East, as a way to legitimise US foreign policy related to the region—specifically Iraq, Afghanistan, and Iran. Middle Eastern characters and symbolism are used as shorthand to denote antagonists and create fear in audiences, and this trend can be unpacked using postcolonial criticism.

Similar techniques have been used in representations of Black people in games, who are often depicted as 'extreme and blatant racial tropes' (Leonard 2006). More specifically, these tropes and stereotypes vary from 'gangstas' to 'sports players' (Adams 2003), which craft Black people into symbols of the 'fears, anxieties, and desires of privileged Western users' (Nakamura 2002: 6). Specifically, this suggests that unless the character is a gang member that can be used to instil fear in a Caucasian audience or a sports player that that same audience can idolise, there is limited motivation to include Black representation in games.

PROTAGONISTS AND WHITENESS

Player-characters in videogames are either predetermined or player-created—which means they are either assigned a race by the developers or the player is given a selection of skin colours and other racial signifiers to choose from (assuming the character is humanoid). Predetermined humanoid protagonists are overwhelmingly white (between 70% and 85%) with a smaller percentage split between being Black, Asian or Pacific Islander, Hispanic and Latinx, Native American, and biracial (Cole & Zammit 2020). This creates a problematic assumption that all players and all heroes are white, or can relate to a white protagonist. Games where there are non-white protagonists tend to have multiple playable characters and present people of colour as options or intermittent player-characters rather than the sole protagonist.

Mafia III (Hangar 13 2016) presents a comparatively rare example of a game with a single predetermined Black protagonist and player-character: Lincoln Clay. The game is set in LA in 1968 and does not shy away from exploring themes of racism by deliberately incorporating interactions between the player-character and his environment that expose the racial politics of the era. By making it impossible for the player to inhabit the life of any other player-character, *Mafia III* forces all players to be exposed to the discrimination that Lincoln experiences as an attempt to elicit empathy or catharsis—depending on the real-life experiences of the player.

Through Lincoln, the player is asked to confront white supremacists, endure racial slurs, and witness hate crimes. The game positions the player as an ally alongside Black NPCs who are experiencing targeted harassment by law enforcement and white civilians by highlighting their shared humanity through shared in-game experiences. *Mafia III* is an open-world game, but the gameworld is not open to Black NPCs—and it's also not entirely open to the player. Hateful glances and comments follow Lincoln through whites-only areas of the map, making him feel as though he doesn't belong. All of these experiences give context to the news reports that the player hears as they drive around the city, including stories about the Freedom Riders and the assassination of Martin Luther King Jr.

Mafia III is far from perfect, but by forcing the player to experience the narrative as a Black protagonist, the game grapples with aspects of racial tension that many games fail to acknowledge. Knowing that all players will be experiencing the world from the perspective of a Black man allows the game to approach the player with a specific form of racial hostility, which games that simply *allow* for a racially diverse protagonist cannot explore. When a character creator allows the player to embody a Black character, the gameworld rarely responds to them uniquely based on the identities that have been selected.

Character creators that feature the bare minimum of non-white skin colours are still limited by the options that a developer provides (Dietrich 2013) and this can result in avatars still being forced to resemble Anglo appearances in some ways, such as through facial features, voice, or hairstyles (Passmore & Mandryk 2018). Alternatively, the player-character might be able to look like a person of colour, but their movements and mannerisms might be stereotypically 'white' (Passmore & Mandryk 2018). This has been referred to as 'digital blackface'—a virtual form of the phenomenon of white people using make-up or paint to make their skin darker and act as a marginalised race (Kaur 2019).

This was taken to the extreme in *Animal Crossing: New Leaf* (Nintendo 2013) when it was first released. Originally, players were unable to customise their skin colour and could only appear dark-skinned if they spent hours 'tanning' at an in-game tropical resort island (Frank 2016), which essentially 'paints' a white-skinned character. With this approach, no characters were able to actually *be* people of colour, even if they were permitted to superficially look like one.

Examining the limitations of character creators through a postcolonial lens shows that 'whiteness' is being used as the default within these systems (Dietrich 2013). Due to the way that media not only reflects but also *maintains* social norms (Harwood & Anderson 2002), existing character creators are thus perpetuating this normalisation of whiteness in future character creators and in society more broadly. It is not enough to take a white character model and allow for the skin tone to be tinted darker; people of colour have more physical and experiential characteristics than the tone of their skin. Ultimately, considering whiteness to be the default for protagonists and player-characters creates a societal assumption that white characters are always the heroes while people of colour are relegated to supporting roles, antagonistic or stereotypical depictions, or are erased entirely.

ORIENTALISM IN THE MIDDLE EAST

In his analysis of the Middle East in fine arts and photography, Said (1978) suggests that the West presents this region as 'timeless and exotic' through orientalism. Although Said's perspectives on orientalism are controversial and oversimplified (Kamiya 2006), Said (1978) is correct in his assertion that people from the Middle East are often incorrectly categorised as a homogenous group. In games, characters from the Middle East tend to belong to one of two stereotypes: adventure and role-playing games exploit 'orientalist' imagery in fantasy settings, while action games and first-person shooters prefer to present Middle Eastern people as villains, expendable enemies, and 'extremists' (Šisler 2008).

Arabian Nights (Silmarils 2001) is an adventure game based on the text *One Thousand and One Nights*, as well as Western stereotypes of Middle Eastern aesthetics and culture. In this game, the player controls Ali, who wears an open vest and a turban. The player moves him through stereo-typical environments such as market squares and palaces, and interacts with characters wielding scimitars or dressed as belly dancers. These 'visual signifiers' are typically used in videogames to ascribe somebody Middle Eastern heritage (Šisler 2008) and are 'effectively props' that are used to indicate that something is 'exotic' to the Western audience (Smith Galer 2019).

Images of 'turbans, fezes, and monkeys' and settings like 'deserts, min-arets, bazaars, and harems' have permeated Western culture because of 19th-century Western art depicting the Middle East (Smith Galer 2019), which used these objects and settings as symbols. These have now become synonymous with many Western representations of Middle Eastern people and culture. The *Assassin's Creed* series (Ubisoft 2018) was heav-ily influenced by this art—particularly the work of British artist David Roberts (Boyes 2018; Martin 2017). Although Roberts differs from many 19th-century Western painters, in that he actually travelled to the loca-tions he was depicting in his paintings, his work still views the Middle East through a Western lens.

The *Prince of Persia* (Brøderbund 2018) franchise assigns the player the role of Western observer of the East, just as Roberts was when he was trav-elling the region. *Prince of Persia* is another collection of videogames that relies heavily on stereotypical visual signifiers to depict Middle Eastern locations and characters, with the series even using the words 'harem' and 'sands' in some of their titles (*Harem Adventures*, *The Sands of Time*, and *The Forgotten Sands*). While NPCs in the game speak with 'caricatured' Middle Eastern accents, the Prince—the player-character—has a distinct British accent, which 'mark[s] him as Westernized' (Tucker 2006). This character acts as a cipher for Western players to project themselves onto. Western mediators are often included in Western representations of the Middle East so that they can proclaim that the scenery is 'strange and/ or wondrous!' therefore establishing the location as 'Other' from the per-spective of the mediator and separating it from the collective Western 'Us' (Tucker 2006).

This Western representation of the Middle East has become so prolific that it has even infiltrated the media of other Eastern countries. *Super Mario Odyssey* (Nintendo 2017a) was created by a Japanese development studio but still borrows from the stereotypes that have been perpetuated by orientalism. In addition to creating a homogenous Middle East, *Super Mario Odyssey* borrows motifs from Native Central and South American cultures, creating open world 'playgrounds' for players to explore that have a mismatch of Aztec, Mayan, and Egyptian aesthetics (Al-Aaser 2017).

Final Fantasy XII (Square Enix 2006)—also a Japanese-developed game—similarly incorporates ideas of the homogenous Middle East into its settings. The game does not map to any specific geographic region; instead, it borrows from many locations to create a 'magical, fantastical East' filled with many of the symbols and tropes mentioned earlier: bazaars, deserts, nomads, silk trousers, hookahs, and so on (Boyes 2018). The game inserts a Western-looking party of characters into this space— including white-skinned, blond-haired princesses and knights (Boyes 2018)—allowing Western players to, once again, project themselves onto these ciphers and have the Eastern world mediated by them.

However, *Final Fantasy XII* also engages with ideas of Western colonisation in a critical—although simplified—way. The game begins in Dalmasca, the name of which alludes to the Syrian city of Damascus, which is in conflict with the Archadian Empire; 'Archadia'—and its capital city of 'Archades'—use word structures that mimic Greek language roots. Archades is aesthetically a Western-looking capital city and characters from the area tend to have English accents (Boyes 2018). The primary antagonist of *Final Fantasy XII* is the Archadian Empire and its leaders, who rule over most of the gameworld. The game's exploration of colonial relations is not particularly nuanced—and does not counteract the problematic homogenisation of the Middle East—but is significant, particularly considering stereotypical representations of the Middle East continue to be used to justify ongoing Western exploitation of the region.

Rather than the 'fantastical' Middle East common in adventure games, action games are more likely to depict Middle Eastern characters as expendable or villainous. This perpetuates modern attempts to make Western society 'fear' the Middle East and thus make US foreign policy more palatable for the Western world—mirroring techniques the media historically used to make colonisation of the East more agreeable to the British public (Höglund 2008).

Homogenisation is also the foundation of these fear narratives, with large groups of people being painted with the same stereotypical brush in order to push a certain agenda. Independent game developer Rami Ismail has spoken on this subject at many industry events. At the Game Developers Conference in 2016, Ismail addressed the homogenous portayals of the Middle East in videogames when he told an audience of game creators that 'Muslim is not a people' (Lee 2016). Despite being a diverse region, people from the Middle East are often assumed to all be Arabic, a term which people also treat as synonymous with Muslim. As such, 'Muslim' has become a 'racialized group' in that it has become associated with particular racial and cultural traits by Western society (Corbin 2017: 458), despite being a term explicitly referring only to followers of the Islamic faith.

This is evident in games when the individual cultures and identities of Middle Eastern settings are incorrectly represented. For example, in *Call of Duty: Modern Warfare 2* (Infinity Ward 2009), the multiplayer map set in Karachi featured Arabic words as part of the scenery despite Pakistanis in this city not speaking Arabic—they speak either English or Urdu. Urdu features the same characters as Arabic, but the words are different—just as many different languages use the letters of the Latin alphabet in different orders and combinations (Boyes 2018; Lee 2016). Even *Assassin's Creed* (Ubisoft Montreal 2007)—which has been praised for its historically accurate and well-researched representations of Middle Eastern cities—makes missteps. In this first entry in the *Assassin's Creed* series, Altair has the same last name as his father (Ibn-La'Ahad), which goes against Arabic naming conventions (Lee 2016).

In addition to blurring the lines between what it means to be Middle Eastern, Arabic, and/or Muslim, Western media has also been responsible for creating an association between the Islamic faith and terrorism. In games, Muslims are 'Othered' by being presented as a threat or linked to terrorist activity, with limited representation of 'ordinary Muslims' provided to contrast with these associations (Šisler 2008). This, in turn, causes audiences to internalise the bias that all terrorists are Muslim or—worse—that all Muslims are terrorists (Corbin 2017).

In action games and first-person shooters featuring Middle Eastern characters, these characters are typically positioned as the 'enemy' and are depicted using an assortment of the stereotypical visual signifiers mentioned above, such as head coverings, loose silk clothes, and dark skin (Šisler 2008). Middle Eastern enemies are often linked to terrorism, with the player-character being part of heroic counter-terrorist forces (Šisler 2008).

The *Counter-Strike* series (Valve 2012) is a first-person shooter with teams of five alternating between offensive and defensive roles. The offensive team is referred to as the 'terrorists' while the defensive side are 'counter-terrorists', who skirmish on different maps that are inspired by different global settings. In *Counter-Strike: Global Offensive*, there are seven terrorist and counter-terrorist 'factions' based on different geographic regions including the Middle East, the Balkans, North America, Somalia, Russia, and Southeast Europe. However, despite the diversity of settings and factions, the 'Elite Crew'—a group of non-distinct Middle Eastern terrorists wearing *shemagh*—receive the most audience exposure. The Elite Crew are the terrorist faction used on 'Mirage', which is the only map that has featured in every competitive major map pool (15 in total), as well as 'Dust 2', which is considered 'the most popular and iconic Counter-Strike map' (Yin-Poole 2017). This means that, although both casual players and esports audiences have opportunities to see a variety of terrorist groups from different backgrounds and with different motivations, they are most likely to see vaguely Middle Eastern people playing the role of terrorists.

When used as villains, Middle Eastern characters are almost always presented as part of a 'monolithic' depiction of Islamic people with no ethnic or religious diversity (Šisler 2008; Deniz & Ismail 2017). When heroic characters or counter-terrorist groups are also depicted as Middle Eastern, they are given more specific nationalities and individual traits. For example, the 'Elite Crew' in CS:GO has a generic 'Middle Eastern' identity but is combated by the Israel Defense Force—a specific organisation from a specific Middle Eastern country. This correlates to wider tendencies seen in journalism and Western media (Hafez 2000; Jackson 2010), but the use of stereotypes to depict all Middle Eastern people as villainous seems to be most prevalent in videogames (Šisler 2008). Portraying individual people as a homogenous enemy group 'trains people to respond similarly to that group of people in real life' (Cole & Zammit 2020).

COLONISATION AS A MECHANIC

Colonisation is frequently explored thematically and mechanically in videogames, from the extremely explicit in empire expansion games to the more subtle in farming simulators. Acts of colonisation are simplified, glorified, and used as mechanics for players to engage with, often without critique.

Sid Meier's Colonization (MicroProse 1995) is an obvious place to start examining the ways colonisation has been adapted to create 'fun' gameplay mechanics, drive in-game goals, and act as a narrative 'wrapper' around design choices that are focused more on their player engagement than political message (Harrer 2018). *Colonization* uses a familiar model of power accumulation as the fundamental guide for the game's design. Players attempt to conquer a larger area and create lucrative trading relationships with Europe, with the 'native' people of America treated as collateral in these attempts to expand. While European people are treated as characters capable of creating new cities, the indigenous people have no agency and are only able to 'wait for Europeans to take advantage of them in trade or obliterate and loot their civilizations' (Owens 2010). In this way, *Colonization* is programmed to consider the European people as characters and the indigenous people as objects or resources—which the player is rewarded for using.

Games that put the player in the role of a coloniser force the player to engage in horrific behaviours and to strip indigenous people of their agency if those games are at all attempting to accurately portray the events of colonisation. However, to remove these horrific actions—or allow the player to avoid them—'whitewash[es] some of the worst events of human history' (Morris cited in Owens 2010). The elements of history that a game conceals from a colonisation narrative can be just as offensive as the elements the game includes. For example, *Colonization* chooses not to incorporate the slave trade into its mechanics despite including many other atrocities committed by European settlers, such as being able to raze indigenous villages or use missionaries to convert indigenous people to then use as labour.

It's a conundrum. Allowing the player to be a coloniser in a historically accurate narrative means allowing—and encouraging—them to commit racist, criminal acts, but removing those acts from the narrative whitewashes history (Owens 2010). Does this mean the only alternative is never exploring colonial narratives in games? Expecting developers to entirely avoid addressing these important historical events in the medium is not a solution either.

BARBARIANS AT THE GATES

Analysing the *Civilization* Series through a Postcolonial Lens

The core game loop of the *Civilization* series (MicroProse, Activision, & Firaxis Games 2019) encourages the player to expand their civilization across a map. As part of this expansion, players are motivated to kill 'barbarians' to gain resources and prevent premature skirmishes. Of the non–player-controlled groups of humans in *Civilization*, the barbarians are granted the least power and significance and are typically removed (functionally, if not literally) from the map early in the game.

The *Civilization* series treats barbarians as unimportant and inconvenient, especially when compared to the civilisations that the players and AI are able to control. Speaking about *Civilization III* (Firaxis Games 2001) specifically, Sybille (2003) notes that settings for 'barbarian activity' are in the menu alongside categories like 'world size' and 'climate', which suggests that the game mechanically considers the gameworld's indigenous people to be more similar to the natural landscape than to the colonising civilisations.

In this settings menu, the primary control a player has over 'barbarian' settlements is how much they can move around the map. This freedom of movement is directly tied to the level of 'danger' the barbarians pose to the player's growing civilization. The highest difficulty setting is 'raging', which relies on the harmful 'savage' stereotypes that have historically been applied to indigenous people to justify their mistreatment by colonial forces. *Civilization III* represents the barbarians as 'a wild tribe which has to be controlled' (Sybille 2003) or—more accurately—eradicated.

However, if we examine the actions of the barbarian units, there are striking parallels between their behaviour and those that the player is rewarded for engaging in. These non-centralised, semi-nomadic people are either performing the same unprovoked acts of violence that the game attempts to justify for the player or are otherwise defending their land against the encroachment of a foreign power who is seeking to tame, dominate, or destroy their home.

The mechanics of *Civilization* devalue any groups that do not explicitly pursue colonial values—not just the barbarians. The city-states that appear in *Civilization V* and *VI* can also be destroyed and pillaged; however, civilizations are also able to form ally relationships with the city-states that are not possible with barbarians, further reinforcing the stereotype that indigenous people are 'savages' who are incapable of interacting with the player through any means other than violence.

City-states lack the innate *need* to expand from where they initially spawn on the map. Their borders will likely grow minutely throughout the course of a game, but they won't create additional cities or attempt to swallow up distant resources. Simply put, they are neither eligible nor interested in 'victory conditions'; they busy themselves with their city's primary interest (maritime, culture, faith, etc.) and are content to watch larger civilisations grow, offering them assistance in exchange for relevant aid.

Unlike city-states, barbarians can spawn additional encampments across the map—even in areas already explored by the player. Barbarians do not use a 'settler' unit to create a new base, which both player- and AI-controlled civilisations require; barbarian encampments will appear anywhere that is currently outside the players' line of sight. This implies that the barbarians are not *founding* new encampments like civilisations do but rather their existing encampments are being *noticed*. This suggests that the gameworld's indigenous people are not using violence as their first act but rather as the only act that allows them to be seen—by the nation, by the player, and by the game itself.

In *Civilization VI*, barbarians can also spawn near cities if the loyalty of that city drops low enough to create disquiet or if an enemy spy agitates a district. By creating a parallel between the rioters or revolutionaries who are reacting to civil upset and the barbarians who otherwise act as tokens of indigenous populations, *Civilization* is allowing the player to view both groups the same way—as an inconvenience that can only be stopped through violent means.

The *Civilization* series features humans gathering together in different types of communities and cities, but suggests that some of these formats are more 'acceptable' than others. Civilisations are treated as the only acceptable way for humans to congregate; only civilisations can 'win' the game while those without colonial motives are ignored, manipulated, or pillaged by the player. This representation fails to question the ideas of colonial conquest that led to European expansion across the world, and which ultimately led to the continuing marginalisation of people of colour.

Resident Evil 5 (Capcom 2009) attempts to address the contention around how to represent colonisation narratives by fictionalising aspects of its story in an attempt to place distance between the player and the horrors they are committing. The game is set in the fictional West African city of Kijuju, where the white protagonist encounters locals who have been infected by a virus and turned into 'bio-organic weapons'. Africa has a bloody history of European colonisation, but *Resident Evil 5* attempts to remove the player's potential guilt around replicating this history and committing violence against the local people by depicting those people as 'infected' and therefore 'framing violence against them as a benevolent deed' (Harrer 2018). But analysing this text through a postcolonial lens reveals that this may be even worse than historically accurate colonisation narratives. *Resident Evil 5* demands that the player kill Black people to ensure the survival of white people, and therefore becomes a shameless representation of colonial domination.

Although the murder of indigenous people is one significant act of colonisation, it is not the only one. Manipulation of landscapes can also be a colonial mechanic in games. For example, games that encourage clearing natural resources, planting introduced species, and building structures—which are core mechanics of many survival, farming, and city-building simulation games (Murthy 2019)—are drawing on colonial ideas. That said, it's important when analysing games using a postcolonial lens to remember that 'scale' is relevant to discussions about colonisation (Murthy 2019). Indigenous people engage in activities like gathering resources and crafting items, but they do this with far less environmental impact than factory production or large-scale industrial agriculture. White violence against people of colour is always an act of colonial violence, but the manipulation of the environment can be interpreted as colonial or not depending on the scale of the action and its impact on the landscape. Videogame mechanics that involve exploiting the environment for the progression of the player are further explored in 'Games and the Environment'.

NON-HUMAN 'RACES'

Similar to the way abstraction is used to create distance between the player and colonial mechanics, abstraction can also be used to explore relationships between different races without directly addressing the political and historical context that exists in relations around white people and people of colour. Some of the most common examples of this stem from Tolkien's conception of fantasy races in the *Lord of the Rings* series (1955), where the 'fair' elves are placed in contrast with the dark-skinned orcs. While elves are treated as noble and beautiful, orcs are treated as irredeemably evil and are 'dealt with by extermination' (Rearick 2004).

The way Tolkien explored race in *Lord of the Rings* and other supplementary texts most obviously influences videogames that directly draw on this source material. For example, *Middle-earth: Shadow of Mordor* (Monolith Productions 2014) explores the tensions between humans and orcs, with the player controlling a ranger named Talion in his quest for revenge against the entire Uruk (Great Orc) population. The in-game description of the Uruks states that they were 'bred for war' and 'hate beautiful things', and suggests that they will approach all situations and people with violence. This description is used as justification for the torture that

Talion is encouraged to inflict upon them. But the representations of the Uruks in the game make it increasingly clear that they are not culture-less savages; they have societal structures and roles, they form bonds and relationships, and they create cultural artefacts to adorn themselves and their strongholds. Not only do the Uruk have language, but based on the lore of Middle Earth, each Uruk can likely speak a local Orcish dialect, the unifying Mordor language 'Black Speech', *and* the common language Talion uses to communicate with them.

The jarring disconnect between the way Uruks are described and how they are actually represented reflects the narratives that the Europeans told as they colonised countries all over the world and claimed that the native people of those lands were uneducated, uncultured savages. These racial relationships—where one is undeservedly treated as 'lesser' than another as a justification for discrimination—are mirrored in other modern fantasy RPGs, with the interactions between fictional humanoid 'races' used as sites to explore real-life conflicts between ethnic groups.

World of Warcraft is a massively multiplayer online role-playing game (MMORPG), with more than twenty playable races across two 'factions'—the Alliance and the Horde. The races within these factions are physically and behaviourally distinct, with their cultural differences being tied to their biology (Monson 2012). This perpetuates erroneous understandings of the supposedly innate differences between ethnic groups when, in actuality, the lines between 'races' are blurred (Tishkoff & Kidd 2004). As Chou (2017) puts it, 'there is so much ambiguity between the races, and so much variation within them, that two people of European descent may be more genetically similar to an Asian person than they are to each other'.

Players are able to join either the Alliance or the Horde and, therefore, are also able to choose how they will interact with other players. Despite this, the Alliance (comprised of humans, night elves, dwarves, gnomes, etc.) are assumed by many to be the 'good' side while the Horde (comprised of orcs, blood elves, goblins, trolls, the undead, etc.) are assumed to be the 'bad' side (Higgin 2009). Initially, little of the in-game lore supported these assumptions, with this instead coming from the players' preconceived ideas of which fantasy races are 'good' and which are 'bad'. It is likely that these assumptions were also influenced by the fact that humans are part of the Alliance, and players instinctively want to assume that people like themselves are part of the morally correct group. These controversial assumptions of 'good' versus 'bad' have since been reinforced by in-game content that depicts the Horde as shifting from a number of groups who unified to ensure their own survival into one clearly defined faction ruled by a bloodthirsty and exploitative warchief.

The representations of the Alliance and the Horde allow players to act out racial relationships and learn from these interactions; however, instead of creating two obviously fictional and morally similar groups, *World of Warcraft* has used fantasy races that have historically been used to depict real-life ethnicities. The game has even reinforced these parallels by drawing on stereotypical imagery and aesthetics in the design of the Horde races (Monson 2012), such as iconography, hairstyles, and facial features typically associated with cultures like Jamaican and Native American (Higgin 2009). When we determine that the 'Horde' is being depicted as the 'bad' faction through player interaction and narrative choice, while simultaneously being the faction that unites races that are aesthetically inspired by people of colour, a postcolonial reading of *World of Warcraft* can show that this game is reinforcing the idea that Blackness is inherently 'lesser' or 'bad'.

All texts are influenced by historical events, cultural iconography, and otherwise *human* stories. Analysing these texts through a postcolonial lens, however, allows us to interrogate the ways that this inspiration is turned into stories that reinforce false assumptions about race, vilify particular ethnic groups in service of a larger political purpose, or glorify and whitewash horrific acts of colonisation rather than critically exploring these continually pertinent concepts.

WHEN ANALYSING A GAME THROUGH A POSTCOLONIAL LENS, ASK YOURSELF...

1. How does the text depict characters of different races, cultures, and religions?
2. Does the text borrow from the aesthetics or narratives of various cultures or ethnicities? How are these used?
3. Which individuals and groups are identified as "Other" in the text? How are they described and treated?
4. How does the text represent the various aspects of colonial oppression, either explicitly or allegorically?
5. How does the text explore the theme of anti-colonialist resistance? Are there ways to resist colonisation within the narrative or mechanics of the game?
6. What does the text reveal about how our race and culture can shape our perception of ourselves, others, and the world in which we live?

CHAPTER 7

Games and Chronic Health Conditions

C HRONIC HEALTH CONDITIONS ARE defined as 'conditions that last a year or more' and that 'require ongoing medical attention' or otherwise impact the daily life of an individual (Anderson & Horvath 2004: 263). This definition encapsulates physical disabilities, neurodivergence, mental illness, and chronic illness and can equally include people who self-identify as experiencing symptoms that fulfil the definition as well as those who have been officially diagnosed with a condition. Although some of these areas of inquiry are recently being talked about more in relation to games, chronic health conditions remain an under-researched field of analysis.

Literary criticism focused on representations of chronic health conditions in texts is still a burgeoning field—particularly when compared to well-established areas of criticism, like structuralism or feminism (as explored in earlier chapters). Growing alongside fields of research like representations of disability in news media (Briant et al. 2011; Johanssen & Garrisi 2020) and educational texts (Táboas-Pais & Rey-Cao 2012; Golos & Moses 2011), the literary analysis that does exist often focuses on physical disability (Hall 2015) or generic 'madness' (Bolt et al. 2012; Donaldson 2002). The lens used for this criticism tends to be referred to as 'disability studies'.

Although mental health conditions and neurodivergence can sometimes be referred to as 'disabilities'—particularly in their more severe manifestations—referring to this analysis as 'disability studies' tends to exclude many chronic health conditions, their symptoms, and their secondary effects as valuable sites of analysis. As such, we will be applying a lens we are referring to as 'chronic health criticism' in this chapter, which we have expanded to include considerations of a broader range of conditions and their impacts.

Although analysing games using chronic health criticism reveals weaknesses, silences, and stereotypes in many cases, some games are actively attempting to explore the stories of people with chronic health conditions and allow these characters to act as protagonists. For example, *Hellblade: Senua's Sacrifice* (Ninja Theory 2017) follows the journey of Senua, a protagonist with psychosis. The creators of *Hellblade* consulted with the Wellcome Trust and psychosis patients to create an authentic representation of psychosis (Takahashi 2019), and, although it was not universally accepted or appreciated (Lacina 2017), it received broadly positive feedback regarding its 'honest' depiction of one symptom of mental illness (Takahashi 2019).

Most of the negative feedback *Hellblade* has received stems from it being one of the only available representations of its kind, particularly in the AAA game space (which Ninja Theory self-identifies as being within (Ninja Theory 2014)). For example, one criticism of *Hellblade* is that the symptoms Senua experiences are linked to trauma and grief; this is not necessarily an unrealistic or inauthentic aspect of the representation but when no other representations exist to provide context to Senua's experience, this can imply that *all* mental health conditions require trauma or grief to exist.

Chronic health conditions can have a variety of causes—or no cause at all—and many of the circumstances that could lead to chronic health conditions in characters are already explored in videogames. However, often the expected impacts of these situations and events are glossed over or erased.

ERASURE

Conditions that last more than a year and require ongoing medical attention are uncommon in videogames. Acute injuries requiring immediate medical attention—such as drinking a potion or sleeping in a bed—are far more common, and typically have no long-term impact on a character. Protagonists can have near-death experiences and return to normal with the application of the correct medicine, with no physical or mental ramifications.

This is in part due to the same 'power fantasy' described in the chapter 'Games and Class', where a continual increase in status and ability is an integral part of the escapist promise many games offer players. When a player-character recovers fully from a life-threatening injury, they are portrayed as strong and healthy; contrastingly, grappling with physical or mental conditions for the duration of a game narrative does not help make a player feel powerful or to escape the realities of their day-to-day lives. This is despite the actions and experiences of protagonists in action-heavy games lending themselves to acquiring physical disabilities or mental health issues. It would be easy to believe that player-characters return from bandit camps, war zones, or ancient tombs with permanent injuries, post-traumatic stress disorder (PTSD), or any number of other long-term consequences, but games rarely explore these topics.

In the trailer of *Rise of the Tomb Raider* (Crystal Dynamics 2015), protagonist Lara Croft is depicted as potentially showing symptoms of PTSD during a session with a therapist (Ishaan 2015). However, this was not included in the game itself, following a public statement made by the game's director who insisted Lara's foot-tapping is not due to 'a weakness or disorder' but rather 'anticipation to get out of the situation and just go on her adventures' (Marco 2015). Despite it being completely reasonable for Lara Croft to be experiencing PTSD or any number of other physical or mental conditions due to her history, the text's creators attempted to not only avoid including symptoms of these conditions but to actively deny their existence, even when plausible symptoms are visible. The concept that a chronic health condition might be a sign of 'weakness' (Marco 2015) is a false perception that relates back to the power fantasy. The idea that people with chronic health conditions are weak and that players want their protagonists to be strong limits their inclusion in games and sometimes causes them to be actively erased from texts.

Similarly, *Metal Gear Solid V: The Phantom Pain* (Kojima Productions 2015) suggests the relevance of chronic health conditions in the title of the game but, although there are several conditions represented within the text, the impacts of these conditions are often minimised or misrepresented. Venom Snake, the player-character in *MGSV*, lost his arm in the 'Ground Zeroes Incident' and—following a nine-year coma and an escape from hospital—is fitted with a robotic prosthesis.

Spotlighting a protagonist and player-character with a chronic health condition is significant, and the game even hints that it is going to explore the difficulties that Venom Snake will experience as he gets used to the new prosthesis; in an early cutscene, Venom Snake has some difficulty trying to take a water canteen from Revolver Ocelot. In a brief exchange between the two, Revolver Ocelot asks if Venom Snake is 'Getting used to it?' and Venom Snake experiments a little with his grip, implying that he is still in the process of adapting to the prosthesis. However, once the player regains control of Venom Snake—and for the remainder of *MGSV*—Venom Snake has no further difficulties or issues. Mere minutes after this stumble, he masters the use of his prosthesis and can roll, grapple, shoot, and climb without fear of imprecision or imperfection.

It seems likely that this representation is intended to demonstrate Venom Snake's legendary ability as a soldier; however, it feels strange that *MGSV* draws attention to Venom Snake's struggle only to ignore it later. Venom Snake's military prowess and near-instantaneous adaptation to his new body creates a disconnect between him and the 'average' person with a chronic health condition, making this representation less about a meaningful exploration of disability and more about the impacts of war.

The multitude of other characters grappling with chronic health conditions in *MGSV* reiterate this assertion. Almost all characters in the text—including minor NPCs—are seen to be carrying the physical, emotional, and/or psychological markers of their experiences with war. Kazuhira Miller, a key supporting character and comrade of Venom Snake, talks about his phantom limb pain and the way it is indistinguishable from—and, indeed, deliberately conflated with—the pain he feels at the loss of his comrades. He tells the player, 'Every night, I can feel my leg... and my arm... even my fingers... The body I've lost... the comrades I've lost... won't stop hurting... It's like they're all still there.' Kazuhira uses both his literal and metaphoric pain to fuel (and justify) his fight against their enemy, again demonstrating that the text is more interested in exploring the cost of war on individuals rather than the lived experiences of people with chronic health conditions.

Relying on chronic health conditions solely to act as a metaphor or symbol is a form of erasure; similarly, using metaphors to stand in for chronic health conditions also erases these conditions from a text. In the *Deus Ex* series (Eidos Montréal 2016; Eidos Montréal 2011), people with augmentations are discriminated against in a way that is indicative of both disability and racial difference without properly addressing either issue. Despite regularly presenting perfect sites for exploring chronic health conditions, games regularly avoid depicting disability, neurodivergence, or mental illness in favour of relying on more typical models of power accumulation. Even in situations where mental health or physical disability are included in games, it is common for these depictions to be downplayed in favour of allowing the player to have fun adventuring without having to think too much about the consequences, or in favour of exploring other issues.

When chronic health conditions are included in a text with limited mechanical or narrative significance, this is considered to be 'incidental' representation (Cole 2018b). This can be seen as a positive way of incorporating chronic health conditions into a game, as people with these varied conditions exist in the real world and are generally involved in actions and conversations that are not explicitly linked to their conditions. For example, in *Overwatch* (Blizzard Entertainment 2016) you can select from a diverse array of characters whose varied appearances and backstories don't impact the gameplay but still provide incidental diversity—including Junkrat, who is an amputee. Similarly, the chef that the player chooses for their avatar in *Overcooked* (Ghost Town Games 2016) doesn't impact the game mechanically but there is the option for the player-character to be a raccoon chef in a wheelchair.

However, depending on its execution, one could argue that incidental representation is also a form of erasure. By making chronic health conditions an aesthetic choice that have no impact on the actions and abilities of a character, the real-life impacts of these conditions are undermined. For example, viewing the aesthetic options in *Sea of Thieves* (Rare 2018) through chronic health criticism reveals that the player-character can equip items that turn them into a stereotypical pirate—complete with hook hand, wooden leg, and/or eyepatch. The incidental representation of these conditions is undermined because the player-character can return to having their original eyes and limbs at any time; these visual signifiers of disabilities are accessories and are not indicative of actual chronic health conditions. NPCs in *Sea of Thieves* also have these visual signifiers of stereotypical 'pirate' injuries but these representations can be interpreted as similarly transient; this gameworld allows the player-character to add or remove disabilities at will, and this implies that other characters inhabiting the same setting can do the same.

All of the characters in *Sea of Thieves* have the same capabilities, regardless of their apparent chronic health conditions. When these conditions are represented in games, characters who acquire serious injuries are often able to resolve these near-perfectly with the right piece of equipment. For example, Bentley in the *Sly Cooper* series (Sucker Punch Productions & Sanzaru Games 2013) experiences an injury at the end of *Sly 2* that causes him to lose the use of his legs; however, in the next game he upgrades a wheelchair so he can still be a secondary field agent and continues to add to the technology of the chair so that the limitations it places on him become inconsequential.

In an even more extreme example, BJ Blazkowicz in *Wolfenstein II: The New Colossus* discovers he has lost the use of his legs. After climbing into a wheelchair, he manages to perfectly navigate a German U-boat despite the fact that several doorways and corridors could not be traversed by a wheelchair-user (Fahey 2020). This is by design—the game's executive producer stated that he wanted to create an 'intuitive' experience where the player would have 'the same freedom as when they are on their feet', which is a game design decision that directly conflicts with the genuine experience of using a wheelchair for the first time (Fahey 2020). Even an experienced wheelchair user would struggle to navigate the space depicted in this sequence of *Wolfenstein II*.

In the *Dishonored* series (Arkane Studios 2017), Billie Lurk first appears as an NPC in *The Knife of Dunwall* downloadable content for the first game and returns as Meagan Foster in *Dishonored 2*. In both of these appearances, she is missing her right arm and right eye but, despite this, manages to hold her own. Billie becomes the protagonist in the standalone expansion *Dishonored: Death of the Outsider*, but by this time her arm and eye have been replaced by 'Void artifacts', which not only return the use of these body parts but actually make her *more* powerful by granting her additional access to magic. Examining this representation using chronic health criticism exposes that the *Dishonored* series does not allow Billie to be a protagonist while maintaining her lost limb and eye, implying that her disabilities needed to be 'fixed' before she could be a playable character.

The representation of Billie's disabilities is an evolution of the idea that videogame characters can have chronic health conditions that don't impact the characters' lives in any meaningful ways. The 'Void artifacts' that Billie uses do impact her life, but positively—by granting her additional powers. Similarly, in *ReCore* (Comcept & Armature Studio 2016) the protagonist Joule Adams has a 'powered leg brace' on both of her legs, which improve her jumping abilities without having any other notable impacts on her life.

This can be interpreted as a form of erasure, with these games ignoring the challenges that come with chronic health conditions in favour of using aids like prostheses as sources of superhuman abilities for the player. However, applying chronic health criticism to these texts can reveal an alternative reading: associating disabilities with superhuman powers presents a source of escapism for people with chronic health conditions, allowing them to experience worlds where they are *more* abled than the average person rather than less. This demonstrates the complexity of textual analysis: there are multiple arguments to be made, and these are capable of existing simultaneously, each equally supported by evidence within the text and secondary sources.

ESCAPING TO IVALICE

Analysing Representations of Chronic Health Conditions in *Final Fantasy Tactics Advance*

Final Fantasy Tactics Advance (FFTA) (Square 2003) follows the journey of several characters through an illusory world that symbolises escapism from their assorted physical conditions and emotional traumas. Ivalice—the setting of *FFTA*—is created when a character named Mewt reads from an old magical book, and the space reflects the desires of the narrative's central characters. These desires vary from healing physical conditions like an inability to walk or white hair, to altering situations that have caused emotional trauma such as the death of a parent, bullying, and neglect.

Ivalice is a manifestation of the concept of escapism. Escapism is considered both a helpful tool and a potentially harmful habit in psychology. Daydreaming can allow us to rehearse future scenarios and avoid danger, solve problems in creative ways, and prompt us to remember important information (Glausiusz 2014). There is a neurological relationship between memory and imagination (Schacter et al. 2008), and escaping into alternate realities can help us establish our identities and integrate ourselves into the outside world (Glausiusz 2014). However, escapism becomes harmful when it is used as a way of avoiding real problems and can also be an indicator of the onset or relapse of anxiety disorders (Spinhoven et al. 2017).

Ivalice represents both the positive and negative aspects of escapism for the main characters of *FFTA*. Marche, the protagonist, acts as a leader in Ivalice and is given attention—which he seems to resist. Experiencing the attention he craved in the real world helps him to better understand himself, and he chooses to use the power of his leadership role to convince others that prolonged escapism is unhealthy and that they should leave Ivalice. For some, it is easy to encourage people to join him on his mission; however, for others, the gifts provided by Ivalice are difficult to refuse.

The main reason Marche received less attention in the real world is because his younger brother, Doned, has an unspecified condition that causes him to be regularly unwell and unable to walk. In Ivalice, his illness is gone and, as a result, he is against Marche's mission to return them to their real lives. Not only does he resist Marche, but he actively stands in his way, reporting Marche's clan to the authorities and alerting bandits of their travels. When Marche and Doned finally confront each other, Doned suggests that it's easier for his older brother to want to return home because there he has 'everything' and Doned has 'nothing'. This oversimplification can be interpreted as erroneously suggesting disability removes everything of value from a person's life.

Ultimately, Marche persuades Doned to help him in his mission to restore their real world by telling him that he envied the attention and love that Doned received—comparing his challenges of being the able-bodied sibling to the challenges that come from being unable to walk. From this conversation, Doned is convinced that his desire to remain in a world where he can walk is selfish. Being a carer or family member of a person with a disability is difficult, but conflating this difficulty with having a disability and complaining about this challenge to the disabled person in question is unfair and damaging.

Doned is not the only character who resists Marche and the plan to return home; Mewt also fights against Marche and his goal of destroying Ivalice. This may be because Ivalice is Mewt's idealised world, so he has even more to lose. In the real world, Mewt's mother died when he was young, and his father became an alcoholic whose struggles at work distracted him from looking after his son. In response to the trauma of losing his mother at a young age, Mewt remains emotionally immature and carries a teddy bear to remind him of her. In addition to being a victim of these life circumstances, he is also victimised at school by bullies.

When a magical book allows him to create an illusory world of his desires, Mewt gravitates towards circumstances that make him feel safe, secure, and powerful. He is made the prince of Ivalice, his mother is alive, his father becomes the 'Judgemaster' whose job is to enforce rules that protect Mewt, and his bullies are turned into mindless monsters. With all of these changes made to improve Mewt's life, it makes sense that he is reluctant to return to his old life as a victim. It is only by demonstrating to Mewt that Queen Remedi—his mother in Ivalice—is actually a manifestation of the magical book that is manipulating him, and therefore once again victimising him, that he can be convinced to work with Marche and the others to return to their real world.

Although Queen Remedi carries the form of Mewt's mother, it is Babus who represents her compassion and love. Although it is not explicitly stated in the text, it is implied that Babus is the manifestation of the teddy bear that Mewt carried in the real world; this is based on Babus's love of Mewt, his role as Mewt's assistant, and the different shape of his nose compared to that of other nu mou (his race). After assessing the situation and determining that this escapism is causing more harm than benefit to Mewt, Babus decides to side with Marche and assist with returning the main characters to their real world. This suggests that sometimes in life, true love is not demonstrated by doting on somebody—as Queen Remedi dotes on Mewt—but through encouraging them to process their traumas, even if that is more difficult than escaping into a fantasy world.

However, the characters still benefit from the time they spend in Ivalice, as this escapism allows them to experiment with danger without experiencing harm. The Judgemaster and his judges enforce the rules of Ivalice—which, mechanically, are reflected in the restrictions placed upon the player in battle. In addition, Judges have the power to heal wounds and prevent death. This means that not only does Mewt desire his mother's resurrection but he has also manifested a world where he never has to grieve the death of another person, indicating his intense anxiety around death and physical injury. This may be based on Mewt's experience with sports or videogames—both of which we see him talking about or engaging in before entering Ivalice—especially because breaking the rules of battle result in a whistle being blown and the character receiving a yellow or red card, drawing a parallel to football.

However, some zones—referred to as 'Jagds'—are not protected by the Judges; in these zones, the rules do not apply, and characters can die permanently. Jagds are mostly optional for the player throughout the game and could be interpreted as spaces for the player to experience the possibility of death in small doses; this alludes to exposure therapy methods used in the treatment of anxiety and post-traumatic stress disorder. Players are better prepared for the Jagds because of their experience battling in safe spaces protected by the Judges, just as individuals can use escapism to practice scenarios while avoiding danger (Glausiusz 2014).

Ultimately, *FFTA* uses Ivalice as a symbol of escapism, demonstrating the positive benefits that people can receive from short periods of time within a fantasy world while also emphasising the harm that can be caused by prolonged periods spent in these spaces. There is a relationship between the escapism represented in *FFTA* and chronic health conditions, as the individuals most tempted to stay in Ivalice are those with physical disabilities, mental health conditions, and emotional trauma; this suggests that people with chronic health conditions are most at risk of being tempted to disappear into fantasy worlds, while demonstrating the harm that can be caused by this temptation.

VILIFICATION

Chronic health conditions can be used as symbolic signifiers that characters or settings are villainous. Some videogames use visible disabilities to denote enemies to the player while others use common symptoms of mental illness in their characterisation of antagonists. Associating chronic health conditions with villains and enemies reinforces harmful stereotypes and social stigma, which in turn negatively impacts the treatment of people with chronic health conditions.

RAGE and *RAGE 2* (Avalanche Studios & id Software 2019) use an exaggerated cleft lip and cleft palate on their 'crusher' enemies, perpetuating a history of clefts being associated with 'villainy and mental health disorders' (Plante 2019). In *Rage 2*, cleft imagery is also used to signify a collection of mutants who are 'subhuman' and 'ridden like horses or mounted like animals' (Plante 2019). Characters in *RAGE 2* are depicted as having fewer physical differences, the 'better' they are, with traditional beauty used as an indicator of allies while physical signifiers like clefts are used to denote enemies.

The *Borderlands* series (Gearbox Software 2019) uses chronic health conditions for similar symbolism, but these problems are hidden behind the praise that the series has received for representations of characters like Patricia Tannis or Sir Hammerlock. Tannis is a character with autism who is integral to the narrative of the original *Borderlands* game and recurs throughout the series. Her representation is nuanced and although her lack of empathy, difficulty with social cues, and other symptoms impact her interactions with NPCs, they are generally accepted by her companions. Similarly, the first character (other than Claptrap) that the player-character interacts with in *Borderlands 2* is Sir Hammerlock, who has an artificial eye. Hammerlock is helpful to the player and is treated with similar acceptance by other NPCs. However, despite these thoughtful representations, the *Borderlands* series falls into the trope of using some chronic health conditions as shorthand for communicating that a character is an enemy.

Just as clefts indicate enemies in the *RAGE* series, dwarfism is linked to villainy in *Borderlands*. *Borderlands* and *Borderlands 2* feature many variations of the 'midget' enemy—a slur used against people with dwarfism. This language was deliberately changed in future titles, replaced by 'Lil' in *Borderlands: The Pre-Sequel* and 'Tink' in *Borderlands 3*; however, replacing an offensive word while continuing to associate dwarfism with villainy does not solve the greater issue with this representation. By positioning people with dwarfism as always being an enemy that the player should kill—and rewarding them for doing so—negative associations are created or reinforced that the player can then apply to people with dwarfism outside of the game context.

The *Borderlands* series doesn't just use physical impairments to indicate enemies. 'Psychos' and 'lunatics' are also common enemies in the *Borderlands* series, named after derogatory terms for people with mental illness. Associating mental health conditions with 'dangerous' characters is not uncommon in videogames. *Batman: Arkham Asylum* also depicts characters with mental health conditions as defective and violent (Lindsay 2014; Dunlop 2018) despite research demonstrating that mentally ill individuals are more likely to be a danger to themselves than others (SANE Australia 2016).

The issues with *Arkham Asylum* are not limited to the characters themselves; the setting of the 'asylum' is a common trope in the horror genre, which suggests that mental health conditions—and the places designed to treat them—are 'worthy of fear, apprehension, and disgust' (Barker 2018). These stereotypical depictions of asylums resemble 'prisons' more than modern treatment facilities, representing mental health conditions as illnesses that require people to be locked up rather than given access to 'practical help' (Cole & Zammit 2020). *Arkham Asylum* is not the only videogame that employs this stereotype; *Darkest Dungeon* (Red Hook Studios 2016) places characters with mental health conditions in the role of player-characters but still relies on the horror aesthetic of asylums—even going so far as depicting the treatment centres as having bars on the windows.

Chronic health criticism can be used to compare characters who are perceived as 'good' with those who are villainous to discover the harmful stereotypes that a text is perpetuating about who can have chronic health conditions. This approach to textual analysis can be similarly applied to setting. When motifs associated with chronic health conditions are used to indicate a character or setting is evil, scary, or otherwise negative, this reinforces harmful associations for the player and can perpetuate or worsen social stigma that already exists around these conditions.

SECONDARY IMPACTS

Where disability studies focusses primarily on representations of disability, chronic health criticism widens the scope to consider all chronic health conditions and how they are depicted in texts. But beyond that, chronic health criticism allows us to examine the secondary impacts of chronic health conditions, both on the individuals with those conditions and on their friends, family, and community.

A study conducted by Golics et al. (2013) found that family members of people with chronic illnesses experience emotional trauma as well as negative impacts on their relationships, finances, and employment. Family members also noted the onset or worsening of their own medical conditions, which Golics et al. (2013) refers to as the 'ripple effect' of illness. This impact is explored in *That Dragon, Cancer* (Numinous Games 2016), where the player is included as part of the Green family and asked to cope with the diagnosis, treatment, and ultimate death of their child, Joel. Joel's real-life parents created the game as an interactive way of documenting their son's cancer treatment, so the game's narrative is told from the perspective of Joel's carers—not Joel himself. This means the story focuses on the various impacts that chronic conditions like Joel's—which lasts for a period of four years—has on the people in his life.

In *Papo & Yo* (Minority Media Inc. 2012), the player-character is also a family member and bystander to another character's chronic health condition. In this case, Quico experiences abuse and neglect as a result of his father's chronic alcoholism, which was brought on by a traumatic experience where he hit a pedestrian with his car. Substance abuse can be a valuable site of inquiry for textual analysis—although it needs to be handled with care, as it is a nuanced topic that can be difficult to appropriately explore within limited scope. In addition to being its own chronic condition, addiction can also be an indicator of other physical or mental chronic health conditions, as well as a range of experiences and traumas. Texts can be more explicit in exploring secondary impacts of chronic health conditions rather than the conditions themselves, so identifying and exploring these secondary impacts—including addiction—can allow for greater applications of chronic health criticism.

For example, in *Heavy Rain* (Quantic Dream 2010), Norman becomes dependent on the fictional medication 'Triptocaine' after originally taking it to deal with physical symptoms caused by the 'Added Reality Interface' system he uses. Similarly, the protagonist of the *Max Payne* series (Remedy Entertainment & Rockstar Games 2012) develops an addiction to alcohol and painkillers in response to the trauma of losing his family (Hamilton 2019; Crecente 2012). In both of these examples, the substance dependency itself is an example of a chronic health condition with its own impacts on the characters and narrative, but it also acts as a marker that draws attention to the other physical and mental health issues that these characters are experiencing and encourages further analysis.

WHEN ANALYSING A GAME USING CHRONIC HEALTH CRITICISM, ASK YOURSELF...

1. Are any chronic health conditions explicitly referenced in the text?
2. How is physical disability represented in the text?
3. How are bodies modified or manipulated in the text to decrease or increase ability? How do modified bodies interact with their environment? For example, does a character receive upgrades that alter their physical body, are prostheses or cybernetics used, etc.?
4. How are acute injuries and illnesses treated in the text versus chronic health conditions? Are characters more likely to experience short-term health issues than long-term impacts?
5. What situations occur in the text that would likely result in a chronic health condition in reality? How are these handled by the text?
6. Can you identify symptoms that might imply the presence of invisible illnesses?
7. Can you identify symptoms that might imply the presence of mental health conditions?
8. How do others respond to characters in the text who have chronic health conditions?
9. How are chronic health conditions used as symbols for other character traits?
10. How do people with or without chronic health conditions relate to concepts of good and evil within the text?
11. How does the text represent places of healing and treatment such as hospitals or asylums?
12. How are secondary impacts of chronic health conditions explored in the text, such as unhealthy coping mechanisms, addictions, financial consequences, impacts on relationships, or caregiving responsibilities?

CHAPTER 8

Games and the Environment

ʿEᴄᴏᴄʀɪᴛɪᴄɪsᴍ', ᴏʀ ʿɢʀᴇᴇɴ sᴛᴜᴅɪᴇs', is one of the most recently developed lenses through which we can look at texts and concerns itself with representations of the physical environment (Glotfelty & Fromm 1996; Barry 2009). An offshoot of ecocriticism is critical animal studies, which looks specifically at the relationships between humans and animals in texts (Shapiro & Copeland 2005; Jański 2016). Unlike approaches to literary criticism that have had decades to develop, ecocriticism is still establishing the key practices and doctrines that comprise it. However, researchers seem to agree that the first step in an ecocritical reading is to focus more attention on the ways texts 'partake in environmentalist discourses' (Backe 2014) and analyse what texts reveal about environmental issues using this 'new dimension' (Barry 2009).

Similar to Marxism, feminism, and postcolonialism, ecocriticism is interested in the power dynamics of society and the norms that these dynamics perpetuate. Best et al. (2007) argue that ecocriticism is not just similar to these theories but must be considered alongside them to reveal 'a larger, interlocking, global system of domination'. This is particularly important in forms of ecocriticism and critical animal studies that believe this lens should not only concern itself with representations of the environment but should also explicitly be involved in the conservation of it (Best et al. 2007; Jański 2016).

Post-structuralism also underpins key ideas of ecocriticism and critical animal studies, particularly in the destabilisation of assumed binaries.

For example, to examine the relationships between humans and nature through an ecocritical lens, first one must establish what 'nature' is. Dichotomies such as 'culture and nature' and 'civilization and wilderness' are socially constructed (Best et al. 2007) and represent a spectrum of human interaction and interference with natural environments (Barry 2009). Similarly, researchers of critical animal studies emphasise that the binary idea of what constitutes a 'human' and an 'animal' is a Western concept, where humans behave as though non-human creatures are their inferiors; this form of analysis seeks to destabilise the human/animal dichotomy (Best et al. 2007; Jański 2016).

The relationships between humans and animals—and where we arbitrarily draw the line—also forms the foundation of a relatively new field of psychological study titled 'anthrozoology', which is beginning to unpack why we have such complicated and nuanced feelings towards animals. Many of the ways humans interact with animals are hypocritical—we invite some into our home as part of the family, we breed and kill some for food, and we use pesticides on others (Herzog 2010). There are some classifications that can be given to different environments and animals in games that help us 'unearth certain patterns related to their functions, origins, and conceptions' (Jański 2016). For example, animals can be depicted as hostile 'enemies' to be killed for experience points and loot, 'background' creatures designed to make the environment more believable, anthropomorphised 'heroes' or allies, 'companions' like pets or mounts, and 'tools' used for transport or resources (Jański 2016).

Different types of animals are more likely to fill different roles. For example, domestic creatures based on actual animals are more likely to be 'tools' while mythical creatures are more likely to be 'heroes'. In videogames, there is also the potential for the player to choose the role that natural elements—including animals—play mechanically by deciding how they want to interact with their surroundings. Videogames present a unique site of analysis for ecocritical readings because their systems are capable of not only representing individual aspects of the environment but also of simulating how ecosystems interact as functioning systems and respond to human influence (Backe 2014).

EXPLOITATION

One of the key sources of study for critical animal studies as outlined by Shapiro & Copeland (2005) are the 'human and animal relationships in the work'—and this can be expanded to examine the environment more broadly through an ecocritical lens. In some games, this relationship can be one of exploitation, destruction, and violence.

Games that focus on the value that animals and the environment can bring to humans or human-equivalents—particularly the player-character—reflect an anthropocentric view of ecosystems. Anthropocentrism positions humans as the centre of the universe and determines the value of others based on their relationships to humanity. Games with an anthropocentric approach to the environment might involve anything from humans being able to freely destroy the environment for necessary resources to humans being able to violently interact with animals for 'fun'.

Minecraft (Mojang 2011) is a game about surviving and creating, and the resources that the player can use for both of these acts are acquired by destroying the natural environment. This environment is built entirely from cubes, which the player can break and remake with various tools. The player interacts with enemy creatures the same way as with rocks: hitting the cubes repeatedly eventually causes them to break and gives you items of value that can be used for your own purposes. In this way, creatures and objects are conflated as similar natural resources in *Minecraft*. The resources the player gains are often used to mirror preconceived ideas of what a landscape should look like, with Western players clearing forests to build roads or neat rows of houses (Harron 2014). This thoughtless destruction of physical space is a type of violence.

The destruction of creatures and the physical landscape is reflected in many survival games where players move through space cutting down trees for timber and killing animals for food. Chickens are commonly portrayed as a source of resources rather than a companion, with their feathers being used for crafting arrows, armour, and quills, while their eggs and meat are used for sustenance (Fothergill & Flick 2016). However, although in these instances players are encouraged to exploit and harm the environment for resources, in some games the value gained from inflicting this harm is more abstract.

Chickens can also be an outlet for violence with minimal or no reward. In *Counter-Strike: Global Offensive* (Valve 2012), the player can kill chickens for a single irrelevant point in 'Deathmatch' mode. In *Fable* (Big Blue Box & Lionhead Studios 2010), the player is able to kick chickens and is given 'titles' for both the distance a chicken travels and the quantity of chickens kicked.

Videogames provide us with an opportunity to examine our relationship to animals, and the way our comfort with exploiting animals differs depending on their species. While kicking chickens for no reason can be incorporated into a game and be considered humorous, players are unlikely to have the same response to the same mechanic being applied to puppies, for example. This disrupts the Western idea that 'human' and 'animal' are discrete categories, instead suggesting that we have different expectations towards different creatures and the ways that they are treated.

COLONISING EVERY NOOK AND CRANNY

Analysing Representations of the Environment in *Animal Crossing: New Horizons*

The *Animal Crossing* series allows the player to live as a human villager in a setting otherwise inhabited by anthropomorphised animals, and *New Horizons* (Nintendo 2020) is no different. The relationships between the player-character, the residents, and fauna and the landscape reveal an anthropocentric perspective where value is given to the environment based on how it can serve humans.

Time passes in *New Horizons* in parallel with the player's real-life time, which is primarily demonstrated to the player through the seasonal changes to available items and the landscape's aesthetic. These changes—like cherry blossoms in Spring or mushrooms in Autumn—encourage the player to pay attention to the environment. With the passing of seasons, different bugs and fish become available on the island for the player to catch and log in their 'critterpedia'. These critters can be donated to the museum for residents to observe or sold to various vendors for a profit. Each creature has a literal value placed upon it, from the cheap moth to the expensive tarantula.

Creatures are treated as synonymous with other objects in the game, like the fossils and paintings that can also be donated to the museum or the fruit and flowers that can be sold to the shop. The mechanic of collecting objects and creatures as though they are synonymous is not unique to *Animal Crossing*; however, it feels especially jarring when the player is catching animals and then donating or selling them to other animals.

New Horizons is aware of this dissonance. When catching a frog, the player-character says, 'I caught a frog! Or it's a new neighbor... and I have some apologizing to do'. This shows that the difference between a critter and a resident is an arbitrary one; there is a line somewhere between 'animal that deserves their own home' and 'animal that can be sold for a profit', but the exact location of this line is not made explicit.

The most obvious differentiation between animals and neighbours is whether they have typically 'human' traits like standing upright, wearing clothes, and speaking a human language. This difference is made most apparent when comparing animals of the same or similar species. For example, the player is able to catch a 'squid' for their critterpedia but there are three 'octopus' residents. Similarly, there are several items that suggest the domestication of animals, such as the 'hamster cage', 'bird cage', and 'doghouse' (complete with chain and collar), but there are also hamster, bird, and dog villagers.

Residents seem insistent on reminding the player-character that they are more anthropomorphised than the critters they share the island with—perhaps because they are trying to avoid being donated to the museum too. As the relationship between the player-character and villagers improves, residents will give the player clothing or furniture, ask to give them nicknames, request help with thinking of new catchphrases, and teach 'reactions'. Each of these emphasises the 'human' qualities of the residents, including their ability to express and share emotions like humans do.

In addition to the variety of residents that can move onto the island, the player-character shares the space with several other regular NPCs. One of these—Isabelle the dog—is responsible for giving the player daily announcements as well as telling the player how they can achieve a better island 'rating'. Isabelle can instruct the player to do several things, including inviting more residents to the island, disposing of weeds, planting flowers, adding or removing trees, and placing more outdoor furniture. If a player wants to achieve a high island rating, they have to interact with the environment in a particular way—which requires them to build houses, clear native flora, and otherwise colonise what was a 'deserted' space.

However, we also know that the island wasn't deserted when the player arrived, as it had a thriving abundance of animals. *New Horizons* simply decides that these animals are somehow 'lesser' than the residents who move in and therefore do not deserve ownership of the island. This mirrors the narratives that colonisers have used to steal land from indigenous people throughout history.

Isabelle's ratings are used to unlock key milestones in the game, including a visit from a famous musician, the recipe for a special watering can, and tools that allow the player to 'terraform' their island. Before terraforming, players are limited in the ways that they can manipulate their physical space; they may dig up trees, smash rocks, or build bridges and ramps, but they cannot make significant changes to the landscape. Terraforming allows players to redirect rivers or block them off entirely, create new ponds or cliffs, and cover whole areas of natural landscape with paths. Tom Nook—the capitalist *tanuki* who is responsible for bringing the player to the island in the first place—encourages this manipulation without consideration for how altering waterways and cliffs might impact native wildlife. For example, some fish can only spawn in ponds or on higher levels, and the player's terraforming might completely remove their habitats.

Animal Crossing: New Horizons is, superficially, a game about the companionship between a human player-character and many animals as they share an island together. However, a closer look using ecocriticism reveals that only some animals are considered equal by the player-character and their neighbours, and what defines this distinction is ambiguous and tenuous. *New Horizons* encourages a positive relationship with the environment as the player watches the landscape change with the seasons, but simultaneously encourages the player to manipulate that landscape to serve their purposes without considering the consequences. Ultimately, *New Horizons* wants players to appreciate the natural environment, but only when it is serving the player's immediate needs and desires, thus promoting an anthropocentric perspective.

COMPANIONSHIP

Games can use companionship between the player and the environment as a way of establishing empathy that can then be applied to their real life. This is often created by anthropomorphising the animals or landscape of the game, and having them assist and support the player.

Talking trees are a common motif in narratives, and games are no different. The 'wise trees' in games like *Dark Cloud* (Level-5 2000), *The Legend of Zelda* series (Nintendo et al. 2019), and *Paper Mario* (Intelligent Systems 2000) assist the player-character by offering advice and guidance and, in turn, foster a positive relationship between the player and the environment.

Games also create relationships between the player and animals. Sometimes this leans on people's existing proclivity towards existing animals, such as dogs, cats, or horses. One of the most common connections created between players and animals is established through the use of mounts which—although used for their utility by the player-character and, in turn, the player—are often treated as friends.

In *The Witcher 3: Wild Hunt* (CD Projekt Red 2015), Geralt and his horse Roach spend more time together than Geralt does with any human companion, and this is shown through the warmth of his dialogue towards her. He tells her stories of his past and is affectionate when giving her instructions, and even jokes about her behaviour and the bugs that sometimes occur when she is pathfinding in the landscape. In a secondary quest from the *Blood and Wine* downloadable content, a woman named Pinastri gives Geralt a portion of a 'common graytop brew', which allows him to temporarily speak to Roach. During these conversations, Roach refers to Geralt as '[her] human' and explains that this is why she can travel to him no matter where he is on the map, emphasising the closeness of their relationship.

Similarly, the relationship between Wander and Agro in *Shadow of the Colossus* (Team Ico 2006) demonstrates their closeness and the time they've spent together. This culminates in a scene towards the end of the game's narrative where Wander must cross a collapsing bridge; despite riding a galloping Agro, it becomes apparent they are not going to make it in time, so Agro bucks Wander onto the platform to safety before falling into the chasm below.

In these examples, companionship between humans and horses occurs by almost anthropomorphising the animals, both in how they are designed and how the player-character interacts with them. The protagonist speaks to them like they can understand—and, in the case of Roach, there is even a circumstance where she can definitely comprehend and respond. This companionship is not reserved for relationships between humans and horses; in *Fallout 4* (Bethesda Game Studios 2015), the player-character finds a german shepherd named Dogmeat early in the game and forms a close friendship with him. After befriending Dogmeat, he becomes one of the player-character's 'companions'—an NPC who is able to follow the protagonist around on their adventures, have conversations, and participate in combat. Other companions become close friends or romantic relationships; placing Dogmeat on equal footing shows the value of his friendship with the player-character.

In addition to animals that are relatively common companions to humans—like horses and dogs—some games create relationships with less typical creatures. *Never Alone* (Upper One Games 2014) follows Nuna and a wild arctic fox as they travel through the tundra, solving puzzles by interacting with the landscape. It is only by switching between Nuna and the fox—or cooperatively playing with a second person who controls the fox—that the player is able to progress. By allowing the fox to either be intermittently controlled by the player or to be inhabited by a secondary player, a deeper empathy of the animal's abilities and contributions to the adventure can be established. The fox is no longer a non-player-character designed only to serve its human companion; it is an equal participant in the journey with some unique skills that are necessary for the pair's progression.

Another game featuring a fox companion is *Yonder: The Cloud Catcher Chronicles* (Prideful Sloth 2017). *Yonder* allows the player to befriend a range of creatures and, although they have fictional names like 'Fernicorn' or 'Girpacca', they are influenced by real-life counterparts like foxes, rabbits, or deer. *Yonder* is an exploration game deliberately devoid of combat mechanics, so interactions with creatures become purely about relationship-building. Although these creatures are able to provide the player with in-game resources, to achieve this the player has to repeatedly interact with a creature, encouraging them to follow the player-character to a fenced area with an always-open gate. Each of these interactions involves the player-character bending down to the creature and touching noses with them, while hearts appear around them both.

The animation shared between the player-character and each creature they befriend are deliberately 'cute' to elucidate affection from the player. Designing for 'cuteness' is a technique used to develop companionship—or perceived companionship—between a person and an animal. Relying on the ways humans relate to creatures they consider 'cute' is an approach animal conservation organisations use to raise money; these groups use mammals with big eyes and fur in their marketing campaigns but share donations with less 'appealing' creatures like reptiles and amphibians (Veríssimo & Smith 2017).

Cute interactions—including the love heart symbolism and rewarding sound effects of *Yonder*—are used in many games to foster companionship. The relationships between humans and animals described so far are just small components of the games they are within, but some games rely entirely on the enjoyment humans feel when forging a connection with an animal. Toys like Digimon and Tamagotchi are designed around the 'human desire to care for dependents' (Anderton et al. 2016) and use symbols of cuteness to encourage players to care about their pixelated pets. The digital game *Nintendogs* (Nintendo 2005) built on the success of these devices, creating an opportunity for players to care for more realistic-looking animals using voice commands and tactile gestures on the Nintendo DS's touch screen.

However, these pets are—by necessity—two-dimensional creatures that do not have the unique and unpredictable personalities of a real-life pet. Interactions with virtual pets also lack the commitment of adopting a real animal, as well as the negative emotions that are an inevitable part of pet ownership—like frustration at misbehaviour, fear of them running away, or grief after they die. Although there may be disappointment at the loss of a virtual pet, it pales in comparison to the loss of a pet that has been integrated into your life for a prolonged period and that you cannot put down and walk away from. In response to this reality, games use techniques like making creatures playable or 'cute' to strengthen the companionship between the player and the environment, which can potentially have an impact on a player's real-life interactions with the environment too.

CONSERVATION

Representations of the environment and animals in some games can inadvertently lend itself towards messages of conservation, while other games explicitly attempt to disseminate this message. Each of the instances of companionship described in the previous section could be argued as contributing to a message of conservation. For example, wise, anthropomorphised trees encourage players to look at the age and wisdom of the landscape and to resist causing it damage. Similarly, using game mechanics to only allow players to have loving and non-violent relationships with wild creatures can inspire people to respond to real creatures they encounter with similar generosity and respect.

Techniques used in these games are utilised in 'serious games' that are created to spread messages of conservation. Serious games are created specifically for a 'purpose other than, or in addition to, pure entertainment' (Barker 2018) and can include games for education and training, marketing, and awareness raising. Serious games have explored a range of conservation topics, including overfishing in *EcoOcean* (Nissen 2015), sea level rise in *Game of Floods* (County of Marin 2019), and sustainable development in *Port of the Future* (de Boer & Vergouwen 2016). Serious games that explore conservation vary greatly in scale and quality, with some being created by experienced development teams and supported by government funding, while others are made by one individual with limited exposure to game-making techniques.

Due to game design's reliance on systems, games present a unique opportunity for players to explore how different actions and interactions can influence ecosystems and natural cycles (Backe 2014), making the creation of serious games for conservation an exponentially growing field. However, it is arguably more interesting to use an ecocritical lens to identify themes of conservation within texts that were *not* explicitly made for this purpose. Just as many games inadvertently represent the environment as something to exploit or as a potential companion, texts can also encourage acts and attitudes of conservation.

Flower (Thatgamecompany 2009) explores the feeling of being powerless in the environment. The game focuses on how individuals may feel unable to 'affect large-scale environmental change' (Harron 2014) and combats these feelings of inadequacy by instead focusing on emotional points of connection between nature and an individual. *Proteus* (Twisted Tree Games 2013) explores a more intimate form of powerlessness, with the player's primary method of interacting with the gameworld being through observation. The player is unable to interfere with the passing of time—even as the winter ends and the player-character dies. By ending the seasonal cycle and the player-character's life cycle in parallel, *Proteus* attempts to establish an empathetic bond between the player and the environment they inhabit, which they are then able to carry with them outside the fictional gameworld.

While *Proteus* is about observing environmental systems, *Equilinox* (ThinMatrix 2018) is about manipulating them. Instead of a first-person camera view, *Equilinox* allows the player to observe the environment from overhead. This suggests that they have been assigned a god-like role, which reinforces the game's primary mechanic: the player can use simplified evolution mechanics to gradually expand and diversify ecosystems. In doing so, the player must carefully place particular flora and fauna together to ensure everything has an appropriate habitat and source of food. Although the game has no explicit win state, the mechanics encourage the player to unlock as many different natural elements as possible by meeting their increasingly complex requirements. *Equilinox* does not explicitly encourage the player to adopt a mindset of conservation, but by showing the ways different species of plants and animals are connected within ecosystems and require each other to survive, the game's representation of the environment incentivises acts of conservation, which can influence a player's real-life attitudes.

An ecocritical approach can also reveal themes of conservation in texts that are not explicitly about natural systems at all. For example, *Cities: Skylines* (Colossal Order 2015) is primarily about urban systems, with the player attempting to establish a successful city that balances the needs of residential and corporate occupants. The challenge of *Cities: Skylines* is the way complex systems overlap with one another, dividing the player's focus. Applying an ecocritical lens to the game allows us to choose one system to focus on and unpack the ways it encourages conservation: the pollution system.

Ground pollution—one of the three forms of pollution in *Cities: Skylines*—is caused by factories, incinerators, and power stations that use fossil fuel. Polluted areas can make individual residents unhappy or sick and can negatively impact the value of land, mechanically penalising the player in multiple ways for investing in power sources that pollute the environment. The game also rewards players for making other environmentally conscious decisions, like implementing policies that encourage the use of electric cars or biofuel buses. These options are just a handful in a game full of large, complex systems, but they encourage acts of conservation by mechanically rewarding environmentally conscious choices.

Ecocritical analysis is not reserved for simulation games either. Observing the *Dishonored* series (Arkane Studios 2013) through an ecocritical lens reveals complicated messages of conservation. In the steampunk world of *Dishonored*, machinery is powered by whale oil and the player-character's abilities are channelled through charms made from whalebone. The relationship between humans and whales is explored in the text, with references to a history where they lived harmoniously existing in contrast with the reality where whales are being exploited for the resources they can provide. The relationship between humans and all animals in *Dishonored* are challenged by similar tensions. The player witnesses both animal abuse and animal attacks during the game, showing that humans and animals are both violent perpetrators and victims in this gameworld. The level of overall violence portrayed is controlled by the player mechanically; *Dishonored* allows the player to complete missions non-violently and, if this offer is ignored, the gameworld retaliates. An ecocritical reading of this mechanic suggests that mistreating the environment results in the environment mistreating humans; for example, the carbon emissions that humans have been responsible for have led to climate change that is now harming humans with heat waves, bushfires, and other natural disasters.

Ecocriticism can be used to analyse any game featuring environments and creatures. This lens is an obvious choice for viewing games that are specifically about ecology and natural systems, but can also be used to reveal interesting messages that are being implicitly presented by games where the environment is not a central focus. Human characters and their experiences are sometimes easier for human audiences to acknowledge and consider; it's important that we don't forget non-human creatures and the environments they inhabit when deconstructing texts.

WHEN ANALYSING A GAME THROUGH AN ECOCRITICAL LENS, ASK YOURSELF...

1. How is nature represented in the text, and what is its relationship to characters?
2. How are animals represented in the text and what is their relationship to characters?
3. How do different characters connect to the natural environment? What do the differences between these characters signify?
4. What environments are present in the text's setting? How are natural and constructed environments treated differently?
5. Are there instances of environmental crisis or disaster represented in the text, either explicitly or through allegory?
6. Where is the environment placed in the power hierarchy? Is nature empowered or oppressed in the text?
7. What parallels can be drawn between the treatment of the environment and the marginalisation of different groups of people?
8. Does the text promote anthropocentric ideas?
9. What purpose do animals serve to the player in the text?
10. How does the text challenge assumed binaries such as civilisation/wilderness and human/animal?

Intersectionality

TEXTUAL ANALYSIS IS A topic often reserved for high school English classes or specific university courses—but it doesn't have to be. Terms like 'liberal humanism' or 'post-structuralism' might seem complicated, but, at their essence, they are just lenses you can look through to see texts in different, more nuanced ways.

There are so many ways to look at the games we play. We can dive deeply into how they explore universal truths, adhere to structures, or represent various identities. We can ask how their systems explore class dynamics or the environment. And—beyond what is covered in the pages of this book—we can ask how designers have created a particular game feel (Swink 2008) or flow state (Csikszentmihalyi & Csikszentmihalyi 1992), how composers have elicited particular emotions in players, or how artists have achieved a distinctive and recognisable visual style. There are hundreds of questions we can ask about each game we play, and no single question is more important than any other. Each helps us to ascribe greater value to the medium by acknowledging the intricate web of decisions, contexts, and values that inform the development of these texts.

Just as there is no single question to ask, there is also no single answer. Textual analysis can lead to multiple arguments being made about any one text, each of which can exist simultaneously and sometimes contradictorily. When we wonder about the impacts that a game can have rather than the intentions of its creators, it's possible to find evidence that supports a range of interpretations. These interpretations can lead to in-depth discussions that reveal the value of games—not just as entertainment, but as an art form.

But the key word here is 'evidence'. Using techniques like those outlined in this book encourages us to conduct research, ask questions, and make arguments that can be backed up with proof that can be found within a primary text (the game) and in secondary sources (other research). Textual analysis encourages curiosity, asking us to apply a range of lenses to the world we live in and unpack the power dynamics that are permitted to thrive there.

Although we refer to these lenses as though they are discrete, and we separate them into their own chapters, it is important to remember that they are fundamentally connected. Each approach to textual analysis was informed by the approaches that came before it and acts as an adaptation, extension, or rebellion. Race does not exist without gender, sexuality does not exist without class, and all of these identities inhabit the environment and are linked by the fundamental questions that make us human. Identity is intersectional.

'Intersectionality' is a term that was originally used to articulate the ways efforts to recognise 'social and systemic' marginalisation often occurred mutually exclusively (Crenshaw 1991), despite the 'multidimensionality' of people's identities (Crenshaw 1989). Specifically, Crenshaw (1991) sought to explore the experiences of Black women and how they occurred at the intersection between existing feminist and antiracist research.

As we look through the lenses described in this book, it is important to also apply the perspective of intersectionality so that we do not accidentally make assumptions about the experiences of individuals simply because they are connected by one dimension of their identities. Even lenses like ecocriticism benefit from an intersectional approach. For example, environmental situations like the Flint water crisis and the Dakota Access Pipeline have been motivated by race and class (Lloro-Bidart & Finewood 2018), and to consider these events without an intersectional perspective erases the experience of marginalised people.

In this way, intersectionality is becoming its own critical lens or methodology. However, we also need to maintain an intersectional approach to intersectionality itself (Bilge 2013). As the term is used more in academic work, we risk creating a prescriptive method for applying intersectionality that undermines other equally valid approaches (Bilge 2013). Academia is a patriarchal institution that serves white straight cis men (Gabriel & Tate 2017), so allowing this institution to dictate how and when intersectionality is used threatens to erase its history. We cannot disconnect intersectionality from its roots in Black feminism.

The idea for this book started while both of us worked at a university, but there is so much value in making supposedly academic concepts more accessible to a wider audience. Textual analysis hasn't just made us better at asking questions about games, but also about the world we live in. We hope this book has helped facilitate that same curiosity and critical thinking for you.

Games Cited

2K Australia and Gearbox Software. 2014. *Borderlands: The Pre-Sequel.* PC: 2K Games.

A.I. Design. 1980. *Rogue.* PC: Epyx.

Ape and HAL Laboratory. 1995. *EarthBound.* Game Boy Advance: Nintendo.

Arkane Studios. 2017. *Dishonored* series. PlayStation 4: Bethesda Softworks.

Atlus. 2011. Original ed. 1999. *Persona 2: Innocent Sin.* PlayStation Portable: Atlus USA.

Atlus. 2008. *Persona 4.* PlayStation 2: Atlus.

Avalanche Studios and id Software. 2019. *Rage 2.* PC: Bethesda Softworks.

Bethesda Game Studios. 2011. *The Elder Scrolls V: Skyrim.* PC: Bethesda Softworks.

Bethesda Game Studios. 2015. *Fallout 4.* Xbox One: Bethesda Softworks.

Big Blue Box and Lionhead Studios. 2010. *Fable* series. Multiple platforms: Xbox Game Studios.

BioWare. 2003. *Star Wars: Knights of the Old Republic.* PC: LucasArts.

BioWare. 2007. *Mass Effect.* Xbox 360: Microsoft Game Studios.

BioWare. 2014. *Dragon Age: Inquisition.* PlayStation 3: Electronic Arts.

BioWare. 2017a. *Mass Effect* series. PC: Microsoft Game Studios, Electronic Arts.

BioWare. 2017b. *Mass Effect: Andromeda.* PC: Electronic Arts.

BioWare and Black Isle Studios. 1998. *Baldur's Gate.* PC: Interplay Entertainment.

Blizzard Entertainment. 2004. *World of Warcraft.* PC: Blizzard Entertainment.

Blizzard Entertainment. 2014. *Hearthstone.* PC: Blizzard Entertainment.

Blizzard Entertainment. 2015. *Overwatch.* PC: Blizzard Entertainment.

Brøderbund, Red Orb Entertainment, Avalanche Software, Ubisoft Montreal, Pipeworks Software, Gameloft, and Ubisoft Quebec. 2018. *Prince of Persia* franchise. Multiple platforms: Brøderbund, The Learning Company, Mattel Interactive, Ubisoft, and Gameloft.

Bungie. 2017. *Destiny 2.* Xbox One: Activision and Bungie.

Camelot Software Planning. 2018. *Mario Tennis Aces.* Nintendo Switch: Nintendo.

Capcom. 1991. *Street Fighter II: The World Warrior.* Arcade: Capcom.

Capcom. 2009. *Resident Evil 5.* PC: Capcom.

Capcom. 2017. *Resident Evil 7: Biohazard.* PC: Capcom.

CD Projekt Red. 2015. *The Witcher 3: Wild Hunt.* PC: CD Projekt.

Cloud Imperium Games. 2013. *Star Citizen.* PC: Cloud Imperium Games.

Colossal Order. 2015. *Cities: Skylines.* PC: Paradox Interactive.

ConcernedApe. 2016. *Stardew Valley*. PC: Chucklefish.

County of Marin. 2019. *Game of Floods*. Tabletop. Accessed 5 June 2020 from https://www.marincounty.org/depts/cd/divisions/planning/csmart-sea-lev el-rise/game-of-floods

Creative Assembly. 2004. *Rome: Total War*. PC: Activision, SEGA.

Creative Assembly and Feral Interactive. 2019. *Total War* series. PC: Electronic Arts, Activision, and Sega.

Crystal Dynamics. 2015. *Rise of the Tomb Raider*. PlayStation 4: Square Enix.

de Boer, W and Vergouwen, S. 2016. *Port of the Future*. PC. Accessed 5 June 2020 from https://www.deltares.nl/en/software/port-of-the-future-serious-ga me/

Dontnod Entertainment. 2015. *Life is Strange*. PC: Square Enix.

Eidos Montréal. 2011. *Deus Ex: Human Revolution*. PC: Square Enix.

Eidos Montréal. 2016. *Deus Ex: Mankind Divided*. PC: Square Enix.

Eidos Montréal, Core Design, Crystal Dynamics, Nixxes Software and Ubisoft Milan. 2018. *Tomb Raider* series. Multiple platforms: Eidos Interactive and Square Enix.

Electronic Arts and Westwood. 2009. *Command & Conquer: Red Alert* series. PC: Electronic Arts.

Ensemble Studios, Big Huge Games, Robot Entertainment, Relic Entertainment, Hidden Path Entertainment, Forgotten Empires, and World's Edge. 2019. *Age of Empires* series. PC: Xbox Game Studios.

Epic Games. 2017. *Fortnite*. PC: Epic Games.

Everything Unlimited Ltd. 2015. *The Beginner's Guide*. PC: Everything Unlimited Ltd.

Firaxis Games. 2001. *Civilization III*. PC: Infogrames.

Freehold Games. 2015. *Caves of Qud*. PC: Freehold Games.

Galactic Cafe. 2011. *The Stanley Parable*. PC: Galactic Cafe.

Gambrinous. 2015. *Guild of Dungeoneering*. PC: Versus Evil.

Game Freak. 2013. *Pokémon X/Y*. Nintendo 3DS: The Pokémon Company and Nintendo.

Game Freak. 2019. *Pokémon* series. Multiple platforms: Nintendo and The Pokémon Company.

Gearbox Software. 2019. *Borderlands 3*. PC: 2K Games.

Ghost Town Games. 2016. *Overcooked*. PC: Team17.

Guerrilla Games. 2017. *Horizon Zero Dawn*. PlayStation 4: Sony Interactive Entertainment.

Hangar 13. 2016. *Mafia III*. PlayStation 4: 2K Games.

id Software. 1993. *Doom*. PC: GT Interactive.

Infinite Fall. 2017. *Night in the Woods*. PC: Finji.

Infinity Ward. 2009. *Call of Duty: Modern Warfare 2*. PlayStation 3: Activision.

Intelligent Systems. 2000. *Paper Mario*. Nintendo 64: Nintendo.

Irrational Games. 2013. *Bioshock Infinite*. PC: 2K Games.

Kojima Productions. 2015. *Metal Gear Solid V: The Phantom Pain*. PlayStation 4: Konami.

Level-5. 2000. *Dark Cloud*. PlayStation 2: Sony Computer Entertainment.

Linden Lab. 2003. *Second Life*. PC: Linden Lab.

Ludeon Studios. 2018. *RimWorld*. PC: Ludeon Studios.

MachineGames. 2017. *Wolfenstein II: The New Colossus*. PC: Bethesda Softworks.

Matt Makes Games. 2018. *Celeste*. PC: Matt Makes Games.

McMillen, Edmund. 2011. *The Binding of Isaac*. PC: Florian Himsl and Edmund McMillen.

MicroProse. 1995. *Sid Meier's Colonization*. PC: MicroProse.

MicroProse, Activision, and Firaxis Games. 2019. *Civilization* series. PC: MicroProse, Activision, Hasbro Interactive, Infogrames, and 2K Games.

MidBoss. 2015. *2064: Read Only Memories*. PC: MidBoss.

Minority Media Inc. 2012. *Papo & Yo*. PlayStation 3: Minority Media Inc.

Mojang. 2011. *Minecraft*. PC: Mojang.

Monolith Productions. 2014. *Middle-earth: Shadow of Mordor*. PlayStation 4: Warner Bros. Interactive Entertainment.

Naughty Dog. 2013. *The Last of Us*. PS3: Sony Computer Entertainment.

The NetHack DevTeam. 1987. *NetHack*. PC: The NetHack DevTeam.

New World Computing. 1999. *Might and Magic VII: For Blood and Honor*. PC: 3DO.

Niantic. 2016. *Pokémon Go*. iOS: Niantic.

Ninja Theory. 2017. *Hellblade: Senua's Sacrifice*. PC: Ninja Theory.

Nintendo. 1981. *Donkey Kong*. Arcade: Nintendo.

Nintendo. 2005. *Nintendogs*. Nintendo DS: Nintendo.

Nintendo. 2013. *Animal Crossing: New Leaf*. Nintendo 3DS: Nintendo.

Nintendo. 2017a. *Super Mario Odyssey*. Nintendo Switch: Nintendo.

Nintendo. 2017b. *The Legend of Zelda: Breath of the Wild*. Nintendo Switch: Nintendo.

Nintendo. 2020. *Animal Crossing: New Horizons*. Nintendo Switch: Nintendo.

Nintendo, Capcom, Vanpool, and Grezzo. 2019. *The Legend of Zelda* series. Multiple platforms: Nintendo.

Nissen, D. 2015. *EcoOcean*. PC. Accessed 5 June 2020 from https://www.eco-ocean.de/play-online/

Numinous Games. 2016. *That Dragon, Cancer*. PC: Numinous Games.

P-Studio. 2017. *Persona 5*. PlayStation 4: Atlus USA.

Pathea Games. 2019. *My Time at Portia*. PC: Team 17.

PlatinumGames. 2009. *Bayonetta*. PC: Sega, Nintendo.

PlatinumGames. 2017. *Nier: Automata*. PC: Square Enix.

Prideful Sloth. 2017. *Yonder: The Cloud Catcher Chronicles*. PlayStation 4: Prideful Sloth.

PUBG Corporation. 2017. *PlayerUnknown's Battlegrounds*. PC: PUBG Corporation.

Quantic Dream. 2010. *Heavy Rain*. PlayStation 3: Sony Computer Entertainment and Quantic Dream.

Rare. 2018. *Sea of Thieves*. PC: Xbox Game Studios.

Red Hook Studios. 2016. *Darkest Dungeon*. PC: Red Hook Studios.

Remedy Entertainment and Rockstar Games. 2012. *Max Payne* series. PC: Gathering of Developers and Rockstar Games.

Respawn Entertainment. 2019. *Apex Legends*. PC: Electronic Arts.

Rockstar North. 2008. *Grand Theft Auto IV*. PC: Rockstar Games.

Rockstar Studios. 2018. *Red Dead Redemption 2*. PlayStation 4: Rockstar Games.

Rocksteady Studios. 2009. *Batman: Arkham Asylum*. PlayStation 3: Eidos Interactive and Warner Bros. Interactive Entertainment.

Sega. 2008. *Valkyria Chronicles* series. Multiple platforms: Sega.

Silmarils. 2001. *Arabian Nights*. PC: The Adventure Company.

Square. 1992. *Final Fantasy V*. PlayStation: Square.

Square. 1997. *Final Fantasy VII*. PlayStation: Sony Computer Entertainment.

Square. 2003. *Final Fantasy Tactics Advance*. Game Boy Advance: Square.

Square Enix. 2006. *Final Fantasy XII*. PlayStation 2: Square Enix.

SNK, Eolith, BrezzaSoft, and Noise Factory. 2016. *The King of Fighters* series. Multiple platforms: SNK, Ignition Entertainment, Atlus USA, Rising Star Games, and Deep Silver.

Sucker Punch Productions and Sanzaru Games. 2013. *Sly Cooper* series. Multiple platforms: Sony Computer Entertainment.

Supergiant Games. 2011. *Bastion*. PC: Supergiant Games.

Superhot Team. 2016. *Superhot*. PC: Superhot Team.

Team Ico. 2006. *Shadow of the Colossus*. PlayStation 2: Sony Computer Entertainment.

Technōs Japan. 1987. *Double Dragon*. Arcade: Taito.

Thatgamecompany. 2009. *Flower*. PlayStation 3: Sony Computer Entertainment.

Thatgamecompany. 2012. *Journey*. PlayStation 3: Sony Computer Entertainment.

ThinMatrix. 2018. *Equilinox*. PC: ThinMatrix.

tri-Ace. 2010. *Resonance of Fate*. PlayStation 3: Sega.

Twisted Tree Games. 2013. *Proteus*. PC: Twisted Tree Games.

Ubisoft. 2018. *Assassin's Creed* series. Multiple platforms: Ubisoft.

Ubisoft Montreal. 2007. *Assassin's Creed*. PC: Ubisoft.

Upper One Games. 2014. *Never Alone*. PC: E-Line Media.

Valve. 2007. *Portal*. PC: Valve.

Valve. 2012. *Counter-Strike* series. PC: Valve.

ZA/UM. 2019. *Disco Elysium*. PC: ZA/UM.

References

Aarseth, E 2001. 'Computer game studies, year one' *Game Studies* 1(1): 1–15.

Adams, E 2003. 'Not just rappers and athletes: minorities in video games' *Gamasutra* Accessed 28 April 2020 from https://www.gamasutra.com/view/feature/131223/the_designers_notebook_not_just_.php.

Al-Aaser, A 2017. 'What games get so wrong about Egypt, 'assassin's creed origins' gets right' *Vice* Accessed 29 April 2020 from https://www.vice.com/en_us/article/wjz544/ancient-egypt-assassins-creed-cuphead-mario-odyssey.

American Cancer Society 2020. 'Key statistics for breast cancer in men'. *American Cancer Society* Accessed 22 March 2020 from https://www.cancer.org/cancer/breast-cancer-in-men/about/key-statistics.html.

American Psychological Association 2020. 'What is exposure therapy?' *Posttraumatic Stress Disorder* Accessed 25 April 2020 from https://www.apa.org/ptsd-guideline/patients-and-families/exposure-therapy.

Anderson, G and Horvath, J 2004. 'The growing burden of chronic disease in America' *Public Health Reports* 119(3): 263.

Anderton, J, Atkinson, M, Berns, F P, Cedillo, C V, Hockenhull, S, Höing, A and Parson, S 2016. *Screening the Nonhuman: Representations of Animal Others in the Media*. Lanham, MD: Lexington Books.

Backe, H J 2014. 'Greenshifting game studies: arguments for an ecocritical approach to digital games' *First Person Scholar* Accessed 11 January 2020 from http://www.firstpersonscholar.com/greenshifting-game-studies/.

Barboza, D 1998. 'Video world is smitten by a gun-toting, tomb-raiding sex symbol' *The New York Times* Accessed 15 March 2020 from https://www.nytimes.com/1998/01/19/business/video-world-is-smitten-by-a-gun-toting-tomb-raiding-sex-symbol.html.

Barker, D 2018. *The Mighty Spoon: Representing Characters with Chronic Health Conditions in Videogames*. Doctoral thesis. University of the Sunshine Coast.

Barry, P 2009. *Beginning Theory: An Introduction to Literary and Cultural Theory*. London: Oxford University Press.

Barthes, R 1957. *Mythologies*, 2012 ed. New York: Hill and Wang.

Barthes, R 1977. *The Death of the Author*. London: Fontana.

Belsey, C 2013. *Textual Analysis as a Research Method*. Edinburgh: Edinburgh University Press.

Bertrand, L 2017. 'Playing with patriarchy: fatherhood in Bioshock: infinite, the last of Us, and the witcher 3: wild hunt' *Proceedings of the 2017 DiGRA International Conference* 1(14).

Best, S, Nocella, A J, Kahn, R, Gigliotti, C and Kemmerer, L 2007. 'Introducing critical animal studies' *Journal for Critical Animal Studies* 5(1): 4–5.

Bilge, S 2013. 'Intersectionality undone: saving intersectionality from feminist intersectionality studies' *Du Bois Review: Social Science Research on Race* 10(2): 405–424.

Blizzard entertainment 2020. Mercy Blizzard Entertainment Accessed 18 March 2020 from https://playoverwatch.com/en-us/heroes/mercy/.

Bolt, D, Rodas, J M and Donaldson, E J 2012. *The Madwoman and the Blindman: Jane Eyre, Discourse, Disability*. Columbus, OH: The Ohio State University Press.

Booker, C 2004. *The Seven Basic Plots*. London: Bloomsbury.

Boyes, P 2018. 'From final fantasy 12 to uncharted 3: exploring gaming's orientalist fantasies' *Eurogamer* Accessed 29 April 2020 from https://www.eurogamer.net/articles/2018-03-24-from-final-fantasy-12-to-uncharted-3-exploring-gamings-orientalist-fantasies.

Briant, E, Watson, N and Philo, G 2011. *Bad News for Disabled People: How the Newspapers Are Reporting Disability*. Project report. Glasgow: Strathclyde Centre for Disability Research and Glasgow Media Unit, University of Glasgow.

Campbell, C 2016. 'Karl Marx and the historical determinism of video games' Polygon Accessed 7 January 2020 from https://www.polygon.com/2016/3/18/11264172/karl-marx-and-the-historical-determinism-of-video-games.

Campbell, J 1949. *The Hero with a Thousand Faces*. Princeton, NJ: Princeton University Press.

Chou, V 2017. 'How science and genetics are reshaping the race debate of the 21st century' *Harvard University* Accessed 31 May 2020 from http://sitn.hms.harvard.edu/flash/2017/science-genetics-reshaping-race-debate-21st-century/.

Chu, M 2019. *Overwatch: Valkyrie* Accessed 18 March 2020 from https://bnetcms-us-a.akamaihd.net/cms/page_media/x3/X38BR3N7HTDP1573261672394.pdf.

Cole, A 2017. 'Playersexuality and plurisexuality in videogames' *Alayna M Cole* Accessed 11 January 2020 from https://alaynamcole.com/academic/playersexuality-alterconf.

Cole, A 2018a. 'Connecting player and character agency in videogames' *TEXT Journal* Special Issue 49: 1–14.

Cole, A 2018b. 'Categories of representation: improving the discussion and depiction of diversity' *Text Journal* 53.

Cole, A and Zammit, J 2020. *Cooperative Gaming: Diversity in the Game Industry and How to Cultivate Inclusion*. Boca Raton, FL: CRC Press.

Corbin, C M 2017. 'Terrorists are always muslim but never white: at the intersection of critical race theory and propaganda' *Fordham Law Review* 86(2): 455–485.

Crecente, B 2012. 'Max Payne 3 is a character study shaped by addiction and violence' *Polygon* Accessed 16 June 2020 from https://www.polygon.com/gaming/2012/4/30/2988059/Max-payne-3-is-a-character-study-shaped-by-addiction-and-violence.

Crenshaw, K 1989. 'Demarginalizing the intersection of race and sex: a black feminist critique of antidiscrimination doctrine, feminist theory and anti-racist politics' *University of Chicago Legal Forum* 1989: 139–167.

Crenshaw, K 1991. 'Mapping the margins: intersectionality, identity politics, and violence against women of color' *Stanford Law Review* 43(6): 1241–1279.

Cross, K 2016. 'Opinion: being sexy and not sexist - a look at Bayonetta and objectification' Gamasutra Accessed 28 March 2020 from https://www.gamasutra.com/view/news/276741/Opinion_Being_sexy_and_not_sexist__a_look_at_Bayonetta_and_objectification.php.

Csikszentmihalyi, M and Csikszentmihalyi, I S (eds.) 1992. *Optimal Experience: Psychological Studies of Flow in Consciousness*. Cambridge: Cambridge University Press.

Dale, L 2019. 'Celeste's creator's silence on their trans protagonist isn't great representation' *SyFY Wire* Accessed 14 April 2020 from https://www.syfy.com/syfywire/celestes-creators-silence-on-their-trans-protagonist-isnt-great-representation.

Dale, L K 2017. 'Zelda, mass effect and horizon all struggle with introducing their trans characters' Polygon Accessed 13 April 2020 from https://www.polygon.com/2017/3/21/15004956/zelda-mass-effect-horizon-zero-dawn-trans-characters.

Deniz, E and Ismail, R 2017. 'Representing the middle East Melbourne' *GX Australia* Sydney, Australia.

Dietrich, D R 2013. 'Avatars of whiteness: racial expression in video game characters' *Sociological Inquiry* 83(1): 82–105.

Donaldson, E J 2002. 'The corpus of the madwoman: toward a feminist disability studies theory of embodiment and mental illness' *NWSA Journal* 14(3): 99–119.

Dunlop, K 2018. 'Representation of mental health in video games' *Connected Learning Summit* Massachusetts.

Dunniway, T 2000. 'Using the hero's journey in games' Gamasutra Accessed 19 January 2020 from https://www.gamasutra.com/view/feature/131527/using_the_heros_journey_in_games.php.

Dyer-Witheford, N and De Peuter, G 2009. *Games of Empire: Global Capitalism and Video Games*. Minneapolis, MN: University of Minnesota Press.

Edwards, J 2013. 'Sand rendering in journey' *Game Developers Conference* San Francisco Accessed 11 June 2020 from https://www.gdcvault.com/play/1017742/Sand-Rendering-in

Fahey, M 2020. 'The wheelchair portion of wolfenstein: the new colossus is some bullshit' Kotaku Accessed 5 June 2020 from https://www.kotaku.com.au/2020/02/the-wheelchair-portion-of-wolfenstein-the-new-colossus-is-some-bullshit/.

Feldman, B 2018. 'The most important video game on the planet'. *The Intelligencer* Accessed 26 January 2019 from http://nymag.com/intelligencer/2018/07/h ow-fortnite-became-the-most-popular-video-game-on-earth.html.

Fernández-Vara, C 2014. *Introduction to Game Analysis*. New York: Routledge.

Fitzsimons, T 2020. 'Lesbians more accepted than gay men around the world, study finds' *NBC News* Accessed 11 April 2020 from https://www.nbcnews. com/feature/nbc-out/lesbians-more-accepted-gay-men-around-world-s tudy-finds-n1118121.

Formby, E 2017. *Exploring LGBT Spaces and Communities: Contrasting Identities, Belongings, and Wellbeing*. Milton Park: Taylor & Francis.

Foster-Harris, W 1959. *The Basic Patterns of Plot*. Norman, OK: University of Oklahoma Press.

Fothergill, B T and Flick, C 2016. 'The ethics of human-chicken relationships in video games: the origins of the digital chicken' *ACM SIGCAS Computers and Society* 45(3): 100–108.

Francis, T 2012. 'We've played the controversial Tomb Raider scene, here's what's really happening' *PC Gamer* Accessed 28 March 2020 from https://ww w.pcgamer.com/weve-played-the-controversial-tomb-raider-scene-her es-whats-really-happening/.

Frank, A 2016. 'Animal crossing: new leaf gives players new shortcut for changing their skin tone' *Polygon* Accessed 10 January 2020 from https://www.pol ygon.com/2016/11/3/13508980/animal-crossing-new-leaf-skin-color-m ii-mask.

Frasca, G 1999. Ludology Meets Narratology: Similitude and Differences between. Videogames and *Narrative* Accessed 7 September 2018 from http: //www.ludology.org/articles/ludology.htm.

Frasca, G 2003. 'Ludologists love stories, too: notes from a debate that never took place' *Proceedings of the 2003 DiGRA International Conference*.

Fron, J, Fullerton, T, Morie, J, and Pearce, C 2007. 'The hegemony of play' *Digital Games Research Association Conference*. Tokyo, Japan.

Fullerton, T 2004. *Game Design Workshop. A Playcentric Approach to Creating Innovative Games*. Boca Raton, FL: CRC Press.

Gabriel, D and Tate, S A 2017. *Inside the Ivory Tower: Narratives of Women of Colour Surviving and Thriving in British Academia*. London: Trentham Books.

Glausiusz, J 2014. 'Living in an imaginary world' *Scientific American* 23(1): 70–77.

Glotfelty, C and Fromm, H. (eds.) 1996. *The Ecocriticism Reader: Landmarks in Literary Ecology*. Athens, GA: University of Georgia Press.

Golding, D and van Deventer, L 2016. *Game Changers: From Minecraft to Misogyny, the Fight for the Future of Videogames*. South Melbourne, VIC: Affirm Press.

Golics, C J, Basra, M K, Salek, M S and Finlay, A Y 2013. 'The impact of patients' chronic disease on family quality of life: an experience from 26 specialties' *International Journal of General Medicine* 6: 787–798.

Golos, D B and Moses, A M 2011. 'Representations of deaf characters in children's picture books' *American Annals of the Deaf* 156(3): 270–282.

Guglielmo, T A 2000. *White on Arrival: Italians, Race, Color, and Power in Chicago, 1890 – 1945*. Doctoral dissertation.

Hafez, K 2000. *Islam and the West in Mass Media*. Cresskill, NJ: Hampton Press.

Hall, A 2015. *Literature and Disability*. Abingdon-On-Thames: Routledge.

Hamid Rao, A 2019. 'Even breadwinning wives don't get equality at home' *The Atlantic* Accessed 20 March 2020 from https://www.theatlantic.com/fa mily/archive/2019/05/breadwinning-wives-gender-inequality/589237/.

Hamilton, J 2019. 'Are video games glorifying alcoholism?' Gamasutra Accessed 16 June 2020 from https://www.gamasutra.com/blogs/JoriHamilton/20190 820/349063/Are_Video_Games_Glorifying_Alcoholism.php.

Hamilton, M 2012. 'Does Tomb Raider's Lara Croft really have to be a survivor of a rape attempt?' *The Guardian* Accessed 28 March 2020 from https://www.theguardian.com/commentisfree/2012/jun/13/tomb-raider-lara-crof t-rape-attempt.

Harrer, S 2018. 'Casual empire: video games as neocolonial praxis' *Open Library of Humanities* 4(1): 5.

Harron, N 2014. 'Fully destructible' *Alternatives Journal* 40(3): 16.

Harwood, J and Anderson, K 2002. 'The presence and portrayal of social groups on prime-time television' *Communication Reports* 15(2): 81–97.

Hawkes, T 1977. *Structuralism and Semiotics*. Berkeley, CA: University of California Press.

Herzog, H 2010. *Some We Love, Some We Hate, Some We Eat: Why It's so Hard to Think Straight about Animals*. New York: Harper Collins.

Higgin, T 2009. 'Blackless fantasy: the disappearance of race in massively multi-player online role-playing games' *Games and Culture* 4(1): 3–26.

Höglund, J 2008. 'Electronic empire: orientalism revisited in the military shooter' *Game Studies* 8(1). Accessed online at http://gamestudies.org/0801/articles/ hoeglund on 28 Mar 2020.

Hunicke, R, LeBlanc, M, and Zubek, R 2004. 'MDA: a formal approach to game design and game research'. *Proceedings of the AAAI Workshop on Challenges in Game AI* 4(1): 1722.

IGEA 2017. 'Digital Australia report 2018' IGEA Accessed 22 April 2019 from https://www.igea.net/wp-content/uploads/2017/07/Digital-Australia-2018 -DA18-Final-1.pd.

Ishaan 2015. 'No, Lara isn't suffering from PTSD in rise of the tomb raider, says director' *Silicon Era* Accessed 24 May 2020 from https://www.siliconera.co m/no-lara-isnt-suffering-from-ptsd-in-rise-of-the-tomb-raider-says-dir ector/.

Jackson, L 2010. 'Images of Islam in US media and their educational implications' *Educational Studies* 46(1): 3–24.

Jacobson, M F 1999. *Whiteness of a Different Color*. Cambridge, MA: Harvard University Press.

Jański, K 2016. 'Towards a categorisation of animals in video games' *Homo Ludens* 1(9): 85–101.

Johanssen, J and Garrisi, D (eds) 2020. *Disability, Media, and Representations: Other Bodies*. Abingdon-On-Thames: Routledge.

Joho, J 2018. 'The "Tomb Raider" movie surpasses gaming's Lara Croft, but is that enough?' *Mashable* Accessed 28 March 2020 from https://mashable.com /2018/03/14/tomb-raider-2018-review-lara-croft-feminism.

Juul, J 1999. *A Clash between Game and Narrative* Accessed 11 September 2018 from http://www.jesperjuul.net/thesis/.

Kamiya, G 2006. 'How Edward said took intellectuals for a ride' Salon Accessed 28 April 2020 from https://www.salon.com/2006/12/06/orientalism/.

Kaur, H 2019. 'This is why blackface is offensive' CNN Accessed 8 February 2019. https://edition.cnn.com/2019/02/02/us/racist-origins-of-blackface/inde x.html.

Keogh, B 2018. *A Play of Bodies: How We Perceive Videogames*. Cambridge, MA: The MIT Press.

Kirkpatrick, G, Mazierska, E, and Kristensen, L 2016. 'Marxism and the computer game' *Journal of Gaming and Virtual Worlds* 8(2): 117–130.

Kirszner, L G and Mandell, S R 1993. *Fiction: Reading, Reacting, Writing*. Boston, MA: Cengage Learning.

Knight, G L 2010. *Female Action Heroes: A Guide to Women in Comics, Video Games, Film*, and *Television*. Santa Barbara, CA: ABC-CLIO.

Korsmeyer, C Spring 2017 Edition. 'Feminist aesthetics' *The Stanford Encyclopedia of Philosophy*. Edward N. Zalta (ed.) Accessed 11 January 2020 from https:// plato.stanford.edu/archives/spr2017/entries/feminism-aesthetics/.

Lacina, D 2017. 'What Hellblade: Senua's sacrifice gets wrong about mental illness'. *Polygon* Accessed 24 May 2020 from https://www.polygon.com/2 017/9/15/16316014/hellblade-senuas-sacrifice-mental-illness.

Lee, N 2016. 'Shooting the Arabs: how video games perpetuate muslim stereotypes' Engadget Accessed 1 May 2020 from https://www.engadget.com/ 2016-03-24-shooting-the-arabs-how-video-games-perpetuate-muslim-s tereotype.html.

Leonard, D J 2006. Not a hater, just keepin' it real: the importance of race and gender based game studies' *Games and Culture* 1: 83–88.

Ligman, Kris 2013. 'Q&A: inside the social futurism of Midboss's read only memories' Gamasutra Accessed 18 April 2020 from https://www.gam asutra.com/view/news/205641/QA_Inside_the_social_futurism_of_MidB osss_Read_Only_Memories.php.

Lindsay, P 2014. 'Gaming's favorite villain is mental illness and it needs to stop' *Polygon* Accessed December 31, 2019, from https://www.polygon.com/2 014/7/21/5923095/mental-health-gaming-silent-hill.

Linstead, A and Brewis, J 2004. *Beyond Boundaries: Towards Fluidity in Theorizing and Practice*. Hoboken, NJ: Wiley.

Linstead, S and Pullen, A 2006. 'Gender as multiplicity: desire, displacement, difference and dispersion' *Human Relations* 59(9): 1287–1310.

Lloro-Bidart, T and Finewood, M H 2018. 'Intersectional feminism for the environmental studies and sciences: looking inward and outward' *Journal of Environmental Studies and Sciences* 8(2): 142–151.

Lo, C 2016. 'How RimWorld's code defines strict gender roles' *Rock Paper Shotgun* Accessed 11 January 2020 from https://www.rockpapershotgun.com/20 16/11/02/rimworld-code-analysis/.

Mandelin, C 2014. 'Is this character in Pokémon X/Y transgender?' *Legends of Localization* Accessed 13 April 2020 from https://legendsoflocalization. com/qa-is-this-character-in-pokemon-xy-transgender/.

Marco 2015. 'Evolving an icon: Lara Croft 2.0' *Tomb Raider Blog* Accessed 24 May 2020 from https://tombraider.tumblr.com/post/123389886680/e3 -ambassador-blog-evolving-an-icon-lara-croft.

Martin, G D 2017. 'Reaching out towards the past in assassin's creed origins' Eurogamer Accessed 29 April 2020 from https://www.eurogamer.net/arti cles/2017-11-05-reaching-out-towards-the-past-in-assassins-creed-origins.

Marza, C 2014. 'Debunking the big myth about transgender-inclusive bathrooms' *Media Matters* Accessed 19 June 2020 from https://www.mediamatters.org/ fox-nation/debunking-big-myth-about-transgender-inclusive-bathrooms.

McWherter, M 2016. 'Blizzard is removing a sexualized pose from overwatch, citing player feedback (update)' *Polygon* Accessed 28 March 2020 from https ://www.polygon.com/2016/3/28/11321138/overwatch-tracer-pose-removal.

Monson, M J 2012. 'Race-based fantasy realm: essentialism in the world of war-craft' *Games and Culture* 7(1): 48–71.

Morris, L 2019. 'Subverting genres: I think I rogue-like you' *GCAP Conference Melbourne*, Australia.

Mukherjee, S 2018. 'Playing subaltern: video games and postcolonialism' *Games and Culture* 13(5): 504–520.

Murthy, N 2019. 'The colonial, non-colonial and decolonial in video games' Gamasutra Accessed 30 May 2020 from https://www.gamasutra.com/ blogs/NikhilMurthy/20190326/339369/The_Colonial_Noncolonial_and_ Decolonial_in_Video_Games.php.

Nakamura, L 2002. *Cybertypes: Race, Ethnicity, and Identity on the Internet.* New York: Routledge.

Niantic 2019. 'Willow report: looming in the shadows' Pokemon *Go Updates* Accessed 14 April 2020 from https://pokemongolive.com/en/post/willow report-loomingshadow/.

Ninja theory 2014. 'The independent AAA proposition' *Hellblade* Accessed 1 January 2020 from https://www.hellblade.com/the-independent-aaa-prop osition/.

Nussbaum, M C 1995. 'Objectification' *Philosophy and Public Affairs* 24(4): 249–291.

Ohannessian, K 2012. 'Game designer Jenova Chen on the art behind his "jour-ney"' *Fast Company* Accessed 23 October 2019 from https://www.fastcomp any.com/1680062/game-designer-jenova-chen-on-the-art-behind-his-j ourney.

Owens, T 2010. 'Sid Meier's: colonization: is it offensive enough?' *Play the Past* Accessed 30 May 2020 from https://www.playthepast.org/?p=278.

Passmore, C and Mandryk, R 2018. 'An about face: diverse representation in games' *CHI PLAY 2018 Melbourne*, Australia.

Pearce, C 2005. 'Theory wars: an argument against arguments in the so-called ludology/narratology debate' *Proceedings of the 2005 DiGRA International Conference.*

Plante, C 2019. 'Rage 2 is a fun game that makes me feel like garbage' *Polygon* Accessed 5 June 2020 from https://www.polygon.com/2019/5/13/18617783/rage-2-impressions-characters-enemies-mutants.

Plunkett, L 2012. 'Gamers "Really Loved Killing" Lara Croft, because she was A "strong" character' *Kotaku Australia* Accessed 27 March 2020 from https ://www.kotaku.com.au/2012/07/gamers-really-loved-killing-lara-croft-because-she-was-a-strong-character/.

Polti, G 1895. The thirty-six dramatic situations *Book Jungle.* (2007 ed.).

Pynenburg, T 2012. *Games Worth a Thousand Words: Critical Approaches and Ludonarrative Harmony in Interactive Narratives.* Thesis.

Queerly represent Me. 2017. *Game Audience Surveys: 2017. Queerly Represent Me* Accessed 26 April 2019 from https://queerlyrepresent.me/resources/survey-results.

Ratan, R A, Taylor, N, Hogan, J, Kennedy, T and Williams, D 2015. 'Stand by your man: an examination of gender disparity in league of legends' *Games and Culture* 10(5): 1–25.

Reagan, A J, Mitchell, L, Kiley, D, Danforth, C M and Dodds, P S 2016. 'The emotional arcs of stories are dominated by six basic shapes' *EPJ Data Science* 5(1): 31.

Rearick, A 2004. 'Why is the only good orc a dead orc? The dark face of racism examined in Tolkien's world' *MFS – Modern Fiction Studies* 50(4): 861–874.

Romano, A 2018. 'Why we've been arguing about Lara Croft for two decades' Vox Accessed 28 March 2020 from https://www.vox.com/culture/2018/3/17/17128344/lara-croft-tomb-raider-history-controversy-breasts.

Ruberg, B and Shaw, A. (eds) 2017. *Queer Game Studies.* Minneapolis, MN: University of Minnesota Press.

Ruppanner, L 2017. 'Understanding the mental load, what it is, and how to get it under control' *ABC* Accessed 20 March 2020 from https://www.abc.net.au/news/health/2017-09-14/the-mental-load-and-what-to-do-about-it/8942032.

Said, Edward 1978. *Orientalism.* New York: Vintage.

SANE Australia 2016. 'Fact vs. myth: mental illness and violence' *SANE Australia* Accessed December 31 2019 from https://www.sane.org/information-stories/facts-and-guides/fvm-mental-illness-and-violence.

Schacter, D L, Addis, D R, and Buckner, R L 2008. 'Episodic simulation of future events: concepts, data, and applications' *Annals of the New York Academy of Sciences* 1124(1): 39–60.

Schreier, J 2012. 'You'll "Want to Protect" the new, less curvy Lara Croft' *Kotaku Australia* Accessed 27 March 2020 from https://www.kotaku.com.au/2012/06/youll-want-to-protect-the-new-less-curvy-lara-croft/.

Schreier, J 2015. 'Why quiet wears that skimpy outfit in metal gear solid V' *Kotaku Australia* Accessed 28 March 2020 from https://www.kotaku.com.au/2015/09/why-quiet-wears-that-skimpy-outfit-in-metal-gear-solid-v/.

Schroyer, T 1973. 'The need for critical theory' *Insurgent Sociologist* 3(2): 29–40.

Scott, C 2018. 'Women's work: unpaid, undervalued and invisible' *Contextual Communications* Accessed 22 March 2020 from https://www.contextu alcommunications.com.au/articles/womens-work-unpaid-undervalued-a nd-invisible.

Shapiro, K and Copeland, M 2005. 'Toward a critical theory of animal issues in fiction' *Society and Animals* 13(4): 343–346.

Shaw, A 2015. *Gaming at the Edge: Sexuality and Gender at the Margins of Gamer Culture*. Minneapolis, MN: University of Minnesota Press.

Shaw, A 2020. 'Locations' LGBTQ Video Game Archive Accessed 18 April 2020 from https://lgbtqgamearchive.com/category/locations/.

Shaw, A, Lauteria, E W, Yang, H, Persaud, C J and Cole, A M 2019. 'Counting queerness in games: trends in LGBTQ digital game representation, 1985–2005' *International Journal of Communication* 13: 26.

Shelton, B A 2006. 'Gender and unpaid work' *Handbook of the Sociology of Gender*. Boston, MA: Springer: 375–390.

Šisler, V 2008. 'Digital Arabs: representation in video games' *European Journal of Cultural Studies* 11(2): 203–220.

Smith, M 2018. *Encyclopedia of Rape and Sexual Violence*. Santa Barbara, CA: ABC-CLIO.

Smith Galer, S 2019. 'How art created stereotypes of the Arab world' *BBC* Accessed 28 April 2020 from http://www.bbc.com/culture/story/2019101 7-how-art-created-stereotypes-of-the-arab-world.

Spinhoven, P, van Hemert, A M, and Penninx, B 2017. 'Experiential avoidance and bordering psychological constructs as predictors of the onset, relapse and maintenance of anxiety disorders: one or many?' *Cognitive Therapy and Research* 41(6): 867–880.

Steinberg, S 2000. 'Lara Croft a living person to creator' *Los Angeles Times* Accessed 15 March 2020 from https://www.latimes.com/archives/la-xpm-2000-oct-26-tt-42072-story.html.

Sundberg, I 2013. 'What is arch plot and classic design?' *Ingrid Sundberg* Accessed 11 June 2020 from https://ingridsundberg.com/2013/06/05/what-is-arch -plot-and-classic-design/.

Swink, Steve 2008. *Game Feel: A Game Designer's Guide to Virtual Sensation*. Boca Raton, FL: CRC Press.

Sybille, L 2003. 'On the border: pleasure of exploration and colonial mastery in civilization III play the world' *DiGRA International Conference: Level Up Utrecht* The Netherlands.

Táboas-Pais, M I and Rey-Cao, A 2012. 'Disability in physical education text-books: an analysis of image content' *Physical Activity Quarterly* 29(4): 310–328.

Takahashi, D 2019. 'How hellblade: Senua's sacrifice changed lives with its thoughtful portrayal of mental illness' VentureBeat Accessed 24 May 2020 from https://venturebeat.com/2019/10/26/how-hellblade-senuas-sacrifice -changed-lives-with-its-thoughtful-portrayal-of-mental-illness/.

The Williams Institute 2019. 'LGBT demographic data interactive' *UCLA School of Law* Accessed 18 April 2020 from https://williamsinstitute.law.ucla.edu/visualization/lgbt-stats/?topic=LGBT#density.

Tishkoff, S and Kidd, K 2004. 'Implications of biogeography of human populations for "race" and medicine' *Nature Genetics Supplement* 36(11): S21–S27.

Tobias, R 1993. *20 Master Plots.* New York: F+W Media. (2003 ed.).

Tolkien, J R R 1955. *Lord of the Rings Series.* London: Allen & Unwin.

Tompkins, J 1980. *Reader-Response Criticism: From Formalism to Post-structuralism.* Baltimore, MD: JHU Press.

Tucker, E 2006. 'The orientalist perspective: cultural imperialism in gaming' Gameology Accessed 29 April 2020 from http://www.aughty.org/pdf/orientalist_perspective.pdf.

Twine, F W and Gallagher, C 2008. 'The future of whiteness: a map of the 'third wave'' *Ethnic and Racial Studies* 31(1): 4–24.

Veríssimo, D and Smith, B 2017. 'When it comes to conservation, are ugly animals a lost cause?' *Smithsonian Magazine* Accessed 22 May 2020 from https://www.smithsonianmag.com/science-nature/are-ugly-animals-lost-cause-180963807/.

Vickery, A 1993. 'Golden age to separate spheres? A review of the categories and chronology of English women's history' *The Historical Journal* 36(2): 383–414.

Vogler, C 1998. *The Writer's Journey: Mythic Structure for Writers.* Studio City, CA: Michael Wiese Productions.

Walker, D N 2016. 'Marginalization and erasure of minority sexual orientations in the LGBT community' *Winthrop University* Accessed 11 January 2020 from https://digitalcommons.winthrop.edu/sewsa/2016/fullschedule/160/.

Ward, M 2015. 'Is structuralism a viable critical lens for roguelike games' *Imaginary Realities* 7(2). http://journal.imaginary-realities.com/volume-07/issue-02/is-structuralism-a-viable-critical-lens-for-roguelike-games/index.html Accessed Sept 2 2018.

Watson, R 2016. 'The ease of progressively depicting "females" in overwatch'. *SkepChick* Accessed 22 March 2020 from https://skepchick.org/2016/08/the-ease-of-progressively-depicting-females-in-overwatch/.

Weiss, S 2018. '7 subtle ways women are shamed for their sexuality on a daily basis' *Bustle* Accessed 29 March 2020 from https://www.bustle.com/p/7-subtle-ways-women-are-shamed-for-their-sexuality-on-a-daily-basis-1001506 8.

Wilson, J 2015. 'Cultural Marxism': a uniting theory for rightwingers who love to play the victim' *The Guardian* Accessed 25 December 2019 from https://www.theguardian.com/commentisfree/2015/jan/19/cultural-marxism-a-uniting-theory-for-rightwingers-who-love-to-play-the-victim.

wundergeek 2012. 'Geek media – what's with all the rape?' Gaming as Women Accessed 18 September 2018 from https://web.archive.org/web/20180915075026/http://www.gamingaswomen.com/posts/2012/05/geek-media-whats-with-all-the-rape/.

Yin-Poole, W 2017. 'Valve updates counter-strike's most iconic map' Eurogamer Accessed 2 May 2020 from https://www.eurogamer.net/articles/2017-10-11 -valve-updates-counter-strikes-most-iconic-map.

Zappone, C 2017. 'Cultural marxism – the ultimate post-factual dog whistle' *Sydney Morning Herald* Accessed 25 December 2019 from https://www.smh .com.au/world/cultural-marxism--the-ultimate-postfactual-dog-whistle-2 0171102-gzd7lq.html.

Index